Gide: a study

Gide: a study

by

CHRISTOPHER BETTINSON

HEINEMANN
LONDON

ROWMAN AND LITTLEFIELD
TOTOWA, NEW JERSEY

ISBN (Heinemann) 0 435 37586 5
ISBN (Rowman and Littlefield) 0 87471 936 4

© Christopher Bettinson 1977
First published 1977

Library of Congress Cataloging in Publication Data

Bettinson, Christopher D.
　Gide.

　Bibliography: p.
　1. Gide, André Paul Guillaume, 1869–1951—Criticism
and interpretation.
PQ2613.I2Z593 1977　　　848'.9'1209　　　76–50073
ISBN 0–87471–936–4

Published in Great Britain by
Heinemann Educational Books Ltd
48 Charles Street, London W1X 8AH
This edition published in the United States 1977
by Rowman and Littlefield, Totowa, New Jersey
Printed in Great Britain by
Richard Clay (The Chaucer Press) Ltd
Bungay, Suffolk

Contents

To Sue

Foreword

This book is intended for the use of students and for the general reader approaching Gide's writings for the first time. A complete list of the French editions used is to be found in the bibliography, and page references in the text are to them. For the general reader, the quotations are translated in footnote, and the list of translations used is also included in the bibliography. Occasionally I have used my own translations and in such cases, the reader will find CDB in brackets after the quotation.

Acknowledgements

I should like to thank Librairie Gallimard and the Société du Mercure de France for allowing me to quote from the works of André Gide, of which they hold the copyright. I wish also to express my thanks to the following publishers for granting me permission to quote from translations of which they hold the copyright:

Alfred A. Knopf Inc., New York, for the American and Canadian rights of *The Immoralist*, *Strait is the Gate*, *Lafcadio's Adventures*, *Pastoral Symphony* and *The Counterfeiters*.

Secker & Warburg Ltd, London, for the British and Commonwealth rights of *Strait is the Gate*.

Cassell & Co, London, for the British and Commonwealth rights of *The Immoralist*, *La Symphonie Pastorale*, *The Vatican Cellars* and *The Counterfeiters*.

I am very grateful to both the University of Glasgow and to University College, Cardiff, who have made research grants available to me which have greatly assisted me in my work on Gide. Finally, I should like to record my indebtedness to friends and former colleagues in the Universities of Reading, Glasgow and in University College, Cardiff, with whom I have enjoyed many fruitful discussions on Gide's work. I should like to thank especially Dr Walter Redfern, Dr Jim Knowlson, Dr Joy Newton, Dr Michael Lerner, Professor Keith McWatters, Professor Austin Gill, and Dr David Bryant.

Gide, the Man and the Artist

Biographical Outline

André-Paul-Guillaume Gide was born in Paris on 22 November 1869. His father taught law at the Sorbonne and was appointed to a personal chair in Roman law in 1872. His uncle was the leading economist, Charles Gide. On the death of his father in1880, André, who was an only child, remained the responsibility of his over-anxious, rather puritanical, mother and her companion, Anna Shackleton.

A very shy and highly-strung child, he had an extremely irregular education. Up to the age of eighteen he had had only three full years of formal instruction at the Protestant Ecole Alsacienne and in two small private schools. The rest of the time he was entrusted to a succession of private tutors in different parts of France. In 1887 he returned to the Ecole Alsacienne, and then spent a year at the Lycée Henri IV preparing the baccalauréat, which he passed at the second attempt in October 1889. He rejected his mother's idea of a Civil Service career to devote himself full-time to his writing.

He had been introduced at a very early age to the pleasures of imaginative literature by his father. He was also a precocious student of botany and music. His enthusiasm for literature was shared, in his early teens, by his cousin, Madeleine Rondeaux, with whom he read aloud from classical and modern writers. It was further encouraged by another cousin, Albert Démarest, who persuaded Gide's mother to allow her son access to his dead father's library. Other influences were the future Symbolist writer, Pierre Louys, who was a fellow pupil at the Ecole

Alsacienne, and a number of young men at the Lycée Henri IV who planned to start a new literary movement.

His first book, *Les Cahiers d'André Walter*, was published at his own expense in 1891. It was much admired by the circle of Symbolist writers, around the poet Mallarmé, to which Pierre Louÿs had introduced him. He subsequently wrote a sort of Symbolist manifesto (*Le Traité du Narcisse*, 1891), a novel (*Le Voyage d'Urien*, 1893) and an allegorical treatise (*La Tentative amoureuse*, 1893).

In 1893 he set off for North Africa in the company of a friend, Paul Laurens. The journey was the expression of Gide's desire to break away from his Puritan background and explore the sexual side of his nature. His first sexual experience with a young Arab boy was followed by an unsuccessful attempt at a 'normal' relationship with a prostitute. Gide's physical education was interrupted when he feared he had contracted tuberculosis, and his mother arrived from Paris to nurse him. By the spring of 1894 he was cured and returned to Paris by way of Rome, Florence and Geneva. Bored with Paris he travelled once again to North Africa, where he spent much time in the company of Lord Alfred Douglas and Oscar Wilde whom he had met also in Paris and Florence. While composing *Les Nourritures terrestres* in 1895 he was recalled to Paris by his mother. Her unexpected death in May released Gide from many of the constraints under which he had always lived, but it also brought him deep grief.

He sought comfort in religion and in the hope that his cousin, Madeleine, whom he had loved since his thirteenth year, would now agree to marry him. After Gide had been assured privately by a doctor that marriage would be an effective antidote to his homosexuality, the marriage took place in October 1895. It was never consummated. Their honeymoon was spent following the route of Gide's North African journey in reverse. On their return in May 1896 Gide was elected mayor of La Roque, a commune in which his mother had left him a property.

Les Nourritures terrestres received a cool reception from the literary critics. Dissatisfied, Gide turned once more to his nomadic existence, wintering in Switzerland, Nice and Rome. Unlike many writers, he played little part in the Dreyfus Affair which had become a major public issue in 1898, although he did defend Emile Zola against Barrès' harsh criticism. While he made many new literary contacts, he remained very much on the fringe of any group. In fact, he hated the official literary world with its theatre parties, earnest discussions in cafés and evening gatherings in the drawing-rooms of the wealthy. He preferred the company of his wife and close friends, or the excitement of assignations with young men on the boulevards and in disreputable cafés.

The hostile attitude of critics to his plays, *Saül* and *Le Roi Candaule*, confirmed once again the small number of Gide's admirers. At the turn of the century he was unknown to the general public and appreciated mainly by the rising generation of writers associated with the three journals, *L'Ermitage*, *La Revue Blanche* and the *Mercure de France*. Thus, the lack of success of *L'Immoraliste* in 1902 – a work which Gide valued highly – inaugurated a long period of doubt and mental paralysis. He had broken with old friends like Pierre Louys and Henri de Régnier, just as he was to lose Francis Jammes and, eventually, Paul Claudel on the issue of his possible conversion to Catholicism. His attitude to his writing did not show much improvement until 1907 with the composition of *Le Retour de l'Enfant prodigue*.

Between 1907 and 1914 Gide completed two major literary projects (*La Porte étroite* and *Les Caves du Vatican*), composed the first two parts of *Corydon*, his apology of homosexuality, and planned with a number of friends the publication of a new literary review. The *Nouvelle Revue Française* first appeared in 1908 under the direction of Gide's younger friends, Jacques Rivière, André Ruyters and Jean Schlumberger, Gide himself preferring to remain in the background. With the launching of this venture and the considerable success of *La Porte étroite* Gide was beginning to find an audience but, even considering the stir caused by *Les Caves du Vatican*, he was to have to wait a further ten years for the general recognition he sought.

During the First World War Gide spent a short time as assistant director of a centre for Belgian refugees. In 1916 he experienced a lengthy spiritual crisis and he also seems to have had a serious difference of opinion with his wife, about which he is characteristically reticent. Whatever the reason, in the following year he began his love affair with Marc Allégret – his first open homosexual relationship – and this was in 1918 to cause a major breach with his wife.

These crucial experiences determined Gide to end the hesitations and self-questioning of the past and make a more direct confession of his nature. This led to the writing of his autobiography, *Si le grain ne meurt* (published commercially in 1926), and the completion of *Corydon* (1924) and the publication of a major study on Dostoevsky. It is, perhaps, also significant that in 1923 Gide was father to a child born to Elisabeth van Rysselberghe, the daughter of a close friend.

After finishing his large-scale novel, *Les Faux-Monnayeurs*, in 1926 Gide travelled in French equatorial Africa with Marc Allégret. In the Congo he noted the exploitation of the native population by the large rubber companies holding concessions from the government. His record of the journey, *Voyage au Congo*, caused a considerable stir in parliamentary circles and led to talk of reform. Broadening his political interests, Gide wrote in favour of judicial reforms, began a trilogy of plays attacking bourgeois marriage and sexual inequality and finally, in 1931, espoused the cause of Communist Russia. His Communist 'adventure' ended in 1936 after a short visit to Russia, and in *Retour de l'U.R.S.S.* he explained his reservations about Stalin's rejection of the ideas that had originally inspired the Bolshevik uprising. Looking back on a decade of commitment to social questions, Gide reflected that he had in fact been denying a natural outlet to his creative powers and had neglected literature in favour of social criticism.

After being reconciled with his wife in 1936, he spent two very happy years with her until her death in 1938. At the time he doubted if he still had the resources to lift himself from the trough of despair into which her death had cast him. Despite their differences Gide had always considered that he loved her deeply, seeing her as a fixed point of restraint to which he could relate the various impulses of his own nature.

The fall of France in 1940 and Pétain's agreement with Hitler came as another profound shock. During 1941 and 1942 Gide published in *Le Figaro* a series of imaginary interviews in which a discussion of literary topics and obscure grammatical points barely hides an anti-Vichy appeal to genuine French cultural values. After two years in the south of France, Gide moved to North Africa where he spent the final years of the war.

In 1946 he published his last great work, *Thésée*, in which the Greek legend becomes the vehicle for a valedictory statement summing up his life's achievement. The following year he received two public honours: an honorary degree from the University of Oxford and the Nobel prize for literature. He remained actively engaged on literary and theatrical projects until just before his death, at the age of eighty-one, on 19 February 1951.

A Creature of Dialogue

Gide's autobiographical account of his early life, *Si le grain ne meurt*, deals with his life up to the death of his mother in May 1895. It is essentially a plea for understanding and an explanation of the complex and often, it seemed, vacillating personality he projected. In particular, it contains an apology of his homosexuality and an assertion that his desire for the physical love of young men is not inconsistent with his sincere, spiritual love for his wife. Gide attempts to show that the origins of his artistic inspiration coincide with the cause of his moral dilemma: both stem from the existence of warring elements within himself. It is only when he can come to terms with that fact that he can serenely contemplate the remainder of his life. Thus, in terms of the title of the book, Gide's new life cannot proceed unless the seeds of his past are truly dead.

At a very early age Gide discovered a perplexing contradiction between his awareness of his own physical nature and the puritanical values inculcated by his mother. This basic situation caused the hypersensitive, much cosseted child to oscillate between the desire to break free and acute feelings of guilt, and to move from one extreme to the other. It was through the confrontation of such antithetical impulses that he moved painfully towards more complete self-knowledge in the direction of fulfilment and serenity.

The key note of Gide's first novel, *Les Cahiers d'André Walter*, is self-denial and wilful renunciation of the flesh. His obsession with an ideal, spiritualized love arose out of his relationship with his cousin and future wife, Madeleine, and was further tested in *La Tentative amoureuse* in which passion is clearly presented as self-consuming and destructive of the will. On the other hand, *Les Nourritures terrestres* preaches an unrestrained joy in all physical experience, now seen as a positive means of glorifying God. Life must be seen as a succession of pregnant moments, each of which should be treated as a wondrous novelty. But self-gratification and egoism have no place in this Gidian vision: on the contrary, what is advocated here is a spontaneous, disinterested joy in creation, involving freedom of movement and the rejection of fixed attitudes and limiting social ties.

Such a tendency to move in an individual work towards one extreme attitude and then in another to draw back from it in a critical fashion is typically Gidian. 'L'œuvre d'art', he wrote in 1897, 'c'est une idée qu'on exagère.[1] Most of his heroes are

---

[1] 'The work of art involves the exaggeration of a single idea.' (CDB)

deliberately presented as logical extremes. In the light of their *hubris*, their *ivresse* or lyrical excess, Gide is able to clarify his own position. It is part of his attempt to bring such familiar impulses under control. In the effort to give expression to a dilemma, Gide strives for a form of detachment in order to illustrate that he has moved beyond the terms of the original moral problem.

However, the control Gide achieves can never be more than temporary. In each new work Gide looks at the same moral and intellectual problems again, posing fresh solutions and seeking new forms of balance. For example, *L'Immoraliste* and *La Porte étroite* have a precise dialectical relationship with each other and, considered together, they illustrate the usual tension in Gide's mind between two opposing attitudes towards life – a tension which few of his early critics could understand. And let it not be thought that by balancing these extremes Gide was hoping to find effective relief from the tensions of his complex nature. In fact, there can be no relaxation and no choice between the two equally attractive impulses that Michel and Alissa embody. The only possible solution – if we can call it that – lies in Gide's ability to convey to his reader an awareness of the problem.

The reluctance to commit himself to any single point of view is seen in Gide's debate with Claudel over his possible conversion to the Catholic faith. Gide's refusal to give in to Claudel's missionary zeal eventually cost him Claudel's friendship. For, what Claudel termed inconsistency and lack of discipline was actually the result of Gide's desire to remain true to his many-sided nature. He was assisted in this desire by a wide variety of friends and correspondents. The problems he debates with one are rarely to be found in his dealings with another and he appears to use his contact with others in a more or less deliberate way to further his knowledge of human nature.

Pierre Louÿs belongs to the period when Gide was an aspiring writer in the Symbolist circle, while Paul Laurens was a key figure in Gide's search for physical fulfilment in North Africa. Gide identified with Paul Valéry's intellectualism and devotion to literature and he shared with Edmund Gosse the problem of his Protestant upbringing. He valued Marcel Drouin's intellectual honesty and for many years treated him as a sort of confessor.

In Francis Jammes and Claudel, however, Gide appreciated qualities quite different from his own, enabling him to define his own moral and religious views more clearly. During the same period he began to form important new friendships. Both Jacques Copeau and Jacques Rivière became close associates because they shared his opinions on literature, and in Valéry Larbaud Gide recognized a cosmopolitan outlook close to his own. In the company of Charles-Louis Philippe he found release from the cultured urbanity of upper middle-class friends like Henri de Régnier and Léon Blum. He appreciated the casual, natural atmosphere Philippe created and relished his new contact with the somewhat racy world of low drinking-houses and the Parisian boulevards.

Gide's relationship with his wife is a special example of his attempt to find acceptance of his contradictory nature in the eyes of another. Looking for understanding and intimacy, all he found was conflict: between her austerity and his desire to explore life's possibilities; between his love of her and the need he felt to express his own individualism. All his works up to 1918 express this basic conflict, albeit in rather ambiguous or oblique terms.

As she is described in *Et nunc manet in te*, Madeleine emerges as the embodiment of the non-physical soul-mate of his adolescence, replacing his mother as the reproving judge of his conduct. For years he shrank from a public confession of his pederasty in consideration of the pain it would cause her and his family. Hence, the first version of *Corydon* was printed privately in 1911 and remained locked in Gide's desk. But after

1916 certain tensions entered into the marriage, culminating in Gide's 'elopement' with Marc Allégret and Madeleine's destruction of all Gide's letters to her. Despite this, Gide was extremely reluctant to sacrifice the possible benefits of a personal relationship simply because of differences of opinion, however deep. Their estrangement did, however, encourage Gide to appeal in the early 1920s to a far wider public in the more direct form of autobiography and treatise.

Gide the Writer

Gide's commitment to his art was absolute and akin to a religious faith. His range was considerable, beginning with his rather self-conscious exploitation of Symbolist themes in his early works and the lyrical fervour of *Les Nourritures terrestres* and moving on to the more tightly controlled classical prose of his *récits* and the burlesque humour and irony of his *soties*. He experimented with every genre – poetry, plays, prose poems, moral treatises, literary criticism, social and political journalism and, above all, novels. In addition, the long correspondences with Valéry, Claudel, Proust, Mauriac, Arnold Bennett and many others add a further dimension to his record of his moral and artistic growth. All of this is also seen in fragmentary form in his assiduously kept diaries, and reconstructed in his auto-biographical works.

Gide was a voracious reader of French, German, Russian, English and American literature. In French literature he showed a marked preference for Montaigne, Pascal, Racine, Rousseau, Stendhal, Balzac, Baudelaire, Flaubert and Hugo. He read Goethe, Schopenhauer and Nietzsche in the original German, learned English in order to read Shakespeare, Milton, Keats, Browning, Blake, Dickens, Hardy, Meredith, Conrad and Stevenson. He read Tolstoy and Dostoevsky, Walt Whitman and Edgar Allan Poe. He translated Shakespeare, Conrad, Rilke and the Indian writer, Tagore, and adapted Kafka for the stage. In fact, he searched everywhere for confirmation of his attitudes and for techniques he might put to use in his own writing.

He is, with Montaigne and Diderot, one of the great magpies of French literature. For him, as for them, plagiarism is the starting-point for a new originality. But to speak in terms of influences on Gide is to pose the question the wrong way round. Gide never sought to acquire, through contact with others, new or 'alien' insights. He always argued that it was a question of 'parenté d'esprit et non descendance'.[1] For example, Gide found in Nietzsche a confirmation of many of his own ideas and ignored what was outside his own experience; and his study of psychology and biology, as well as his analysis of his own nervous disorders, put him in touch with 'Freudian' ideas long before he read Freud.

His communion with other writers and his frequent use of quotation, foreign phrases and technical vocabulary often gave rise to the charge that he was excessively pedantic and not sufficiently personal in his style. Gide had frequently to explain himself on this point. He prefers his own honesty to the subterfuge of those who try to hide their sources, and he loves to present his detractors with proof that he is not unique in some of his more provocative ideas. In addition, there is a stylistic significance. As with Montaigne, they are not merely decorative excrescences: such quotations or *bons mots* strike his attention because they seem to be the *best* expression of a certain idea. These formulae find their way into Gide's diary only to turn up with little or no modification in later works. The procedure is analogous with the way in which, in *Les Caves du Vatican*, there are many precise echoes of passages in earlier works.[2]

The language Gide uses is not that of the philosopher or the

[1] 'Intellectual kinship and not descent.' (CDB)
[2] See A. Goulet, *Les Caves du Vatican d'André Gide* . . . Larousse, 1972, pp. 41–78.

psychologist but that of the creative artist, and in his search for a new originality Gide was acutely aware of the limitations of conventional language and syntax. Hence the never-ending experimentation with form and linguistic structure and the careful documentation from all sources. The search for new forms combines with attempts to stretch the capabilities of the language he inherited, resurrecting archaic words and grammatical structures, and finding room for all kinds of popular expressions, so that we end up with a lively mixture of the colloquial and the refined.

Working against this tendency towards linguistic exuberance is an equally powerful impulse for clarity, sobriety and control. Gide's works matured in his mind for many years before he was able to reach the stage of composition. But despite this hesitation and obsessive desire for precision, Gide set great store during the composition of his works, by the involuntary and spontaneous workings of his mind. Allowing his mind to wander freely, Gide suddenly becomes aware of an idea. At this point it becomes necessary to carefully reconstruct the mental processes by which his mind has reached the new idea. The aim, of course, is to create an art that has all the appearances of artlessness – to rival the impression of naturalness he admired so much in Stendhal and de Retz.

Gide's writing was experimental in a number of ways: he tested ideas in a variety of conditions; he subjected his linguistic equipment to ceaseless scrutiny and he experimented with many different styles and genres. But perhaps his main achievement lies in his thinking on the novel, based on his reactions to nineteenth-century realism. His Symbolist experience taught that it is the artist's duty to transcend the meaningless details of everyday reality. The work of art is a closed system of linguistic signs – an artificial world. While it will certainly suggest human truths and encapsulate human experience, it must never reflect life in a banal, descriptive way. In fact, a novel can only illustrate the complexity of life if the artist abandons any attempt to be a neutral observer and projects instead the uniqueness of his own point of view. By a heavy concentration on the particular truth, the artist can make it symbolize a universal truth even more forcefully.

In literature it is not so much a question of what truth is as what the artist can persuade his readers to believe. Fiction may often seem unreal, but then, truth may often seem stranger than fiction: in neither case is the possible human significance at issue. Style, and literary convention which sometimes creates an impression of artificiality, provides an essential distancing effect that enables the human truths to emerge all the more clearly. Hence Gide's admiration for Racinian tragedy which, while it is obviously more formalized than Shakespeare's, still maintains its powerful human significance.

Gide was constantly alluding to the question of the relationship between literature and life. One of his favourite techniques is the first-person narrative convention, which he uses to approach reality from an oblique angle. Superficially, he deliberately absents himself from the action of his works, creating the impression that his narrator-heroes are free to express their own view of reality. But as the reader becomes aware of the extreme partiality of the self-justifying narrator, a new critical viewpoint comes into play, constantly judging and modifying the narrator's account of his life. This is the case in the four *récits*, *L'Immoraliste*, *La Porte étroite*, *Isabelle* and *La Symphonie pastorale*. In *Les Caves du Vatican*, however, Gide apparently liberates all of the characters from the viewpoint of a narrator-hero, thus giving the impression of a many-sided reality. In the clash of these different points of view, Gide hoped to suggest, rather in the manner of Fielding and Sterne, the almost irreducible complexities of life.

Another technique is to place in individual works characters whose own literary preoccupations mirror Gide's own objectives in the work. *Les Cahiers d'André Walter* is the story of a young man trying to write a novel called *Alain*; *Paludes* comments critically on the problems faced by a man writing a novel of the same name. This technique is repeated in *Les Caves du Vatican* and brought to perfection in *Les Faux-Monnayeurs*, which is full of characters who are aspiring writers, including the novelist, Edouard, around whom the action pivots.

Gide makes the novel the focal point of different versions of reality. Events are not related directly but through a succession of partial viewpoints and it is the role of the reader to relate them to each other. Gide's reader must be prepared to follow him in his quest for new forms and assist in the creation of a multi-dimensional experience of life seen in the round. For Gide the role of the artist was to stimulate creative thought, to pose problems and not to present ready-made solutions. By itself a work of art has only a *potential* significance: it acquires its full status only when it is read, interpreted and experienced by a reader:

> Avant d'expliquer aux autres mon livre, j'attends que d'autres me l'expliquent.[1]

---

[1] 'Before explaining my book to others, I wait for them to explain it to me.' (CDB)

2

L'Immoraliste and *La Porte étroite*

L'Immoraliste and *La Porte étroite* are both *récits*. Longer than short stories, shorter and less complex than the conventional novel, they are critical or ironical works, each concentrating on one particular aspect of life, related directly by one of the principal protagonists. They are marked by a kind of ironic detachment fostered by the simplicity of plot, an extreme economy of stylistic means and a relentless narrative rhythm, which emphasizes the tragic destinies of both Michel and Alissa. The reader is invited to sympathize with them and, at the same time, view them critically as they involve others in the implacable logic of their extremism.

Taken together, then, *La Porte étroite* and *L'Immoraliste* create a balance between opposing attitudes to life, each taken to a logical extreme. In the latter, Gide's fascination for individual, natural impulses is sympathetically examined and countered by a less sympathetic but realistic awareness of social demands. In *La Porte étroite*, on the other hand, Gide approaches the same social demands from the point of view of an attitude of extreme self-sacrifice, embodied in Alissa. Ultimately, a ferocious attachment to physical fulfilment is balanced against an equally strong impulse towards self-abnegation.

L'Immoraliste

L'Immoraliste is divided into three unequal parts. The long first part, composed of nine chapters, is set in North Africa and charts Michel's slow recovery from tuberculosis, through the exercise of his will and his discovery of the world of the senses. This culminates in the consummation of his relationship with his wife and in the apparent establishment of a new balance in his life. Part Two consists of three long chapters, set in La Morinière, Paris, and back in La Morinière, in which Michel's marriage and his growing obsession for physical experience are seen in conflict. A significant encounter with Ménalque in the central chapter encourages Michel in his search for new experience, now clearly seen as incompatible with his responsibilities as husband and landowner. Part Three describes Michel's failure to revive the earlier intensity of his love for Marceline and his constant neglect of her needs as he systematically searches for physical satisfaction. With Marceline's death, the inevitable consequence of Michel's personal quest, he finds himself committed to his immoralism but without the will and energy to cultivate it.

The introductory letter (pp. 13–16)[1] provides a dramatic introduction to Michel's tale. The suggestive use of questions, the deliberately broken rhythm and the hesitancy of the writer combine to produce a sense of urgency and moment. This is reinforced by the repeated movement from the brief, factual details concerning the arrival of Michel's visitors towards hints of Michel's predicament that are tantalizingly cut short with *points de suspension*. In addition, the situation of the house overlooking the plain and the fact that the story is told on 'la terrasse d'où la vue à l'infini s'étendait' (p. 16)[2] have symbolic overtones. There is an all-pervading sense of solemnity and silent expectation as day turns to night and scarcely a word is exchanged.

Michel's promise to tell his story 'simplement, sans modestie et sans orgueil' (p. 16)[3] is borne out in his brutally frank

---

[1] pp. 9–11. (Page references in footnotes are to the English translation, the French editions used are listed in the Bibliography.)

[2] 'the terrace, where the view stretched away into infinity'. (p. 11)

[3] 'simply, without modesty and without pride'. (p. 13)

explanation of his superficial love for Marceline in terms of his sheltered Puritan upbringing and his ignorance of life in general. It is important to remember that, as in all autobiographical fiction, ambiguity arises from the confusion between the attempt at an honest record of past events and the inevitable structuring and justification of the past in the light of subsequent experience. Thus the unmistakable callousness of most references to Marceline throughout the book seems to be an exaggeration of Michel's vague feelings in the past, conditioned by his present knowledge of where such feelings were in fact leading him.

The onset of illness leads Michel to become more aware of Marceline's beauty and her physical reality, but at the same time her response to his illness irritates him. She faints when he casually tells her that he has coughed up blood, her feverish concern for his well-being nearly brings him to the point of death and, when Michel resolves to cure himself by an act of will, there is tremendous emphasis on his self-sufficiency, leading him to reject the prayers she offers on his behalf. In this there is already the implication that Michel is proposing unwittingly a new scale of moral values.

> Je repassais ma volonté comme une leçon qu'on repasse; j'apprenais mon hostilité, la dirigeais sur toutes choses; je devais lutter contre tout: mon salut dépendait de moi seul. (p. 38)[1]

Marceline's exclusion from Michel's self-directed recuperation is seen in the private communion Michel has with the natural world even when Marceline is present (chapter four) and in his attraction for a rival group of healthy Arab boys, whereas 'ceux que Marceline choyait étaient faibles, chétifs, et trop

---

[1] I strengthened my will as one strengthens one's memory by revising a lesson; I instructed my hostility, directed it against all and sundry; I was to fight with everything; my salvation depended on myself alone. (p. 31)

sages' (p. 53).[1] Finally, it is epitomized in Michel's complicity with Moktir over the incident of the missing scissors.

Gide remains slightly equivocal about Michel's discovery of the world of physical sensation. In a number of brilliantly lyrical passages in chapters three, four and five he stresses the tonic value of this new contact with nature and, at the same time, suggests a dangerous tendency towards excess:

> Cette terre africaine, dont je ne connaissais pas l'attente, submergée durant de longs jours, à present s'éveillait de l'hiver, ivre d'eau, éclatant de sèves nouvelles; elle riait d'un printemps forcené dont je sentais le retentissement et comme le double en moi-même. (pp. 55-6)[2]

And, despite Michel's good intentions towards Marceline and his premonition of his tragic destiny at the end of chapter five, he becomes obsessed with his search for physical fitness and is involved in a successful trial of strength with the drunken coachman in chapter eight in order to protect Marceline. But already a new philosophy of life has been defined in relation to the past (chapter six) and this is symbolized in Michel's fascination for the savagery of Athalaric the Goth (chapter nine).

At the peak of his physical powers, Michel makes love to Marceline for the first time, but his feelings to her remain ambivalent. On her behalf he plays a role that is clearly at variance with his deeper feelings. This is seen in his dissembling behaviour in chapter seven and in his sense of guilt that prompts him, for Marceline's sake, to attempt to reconcile his new ethical philosophy and his abandoned academic career (chapter

---

[1] 'Those that Marceline petted were weakly, sickly, and too well-behaved'. (p. 44)

[2] This African land, whose thirsty season of waiting was not then known to me, had lain submerged for many long days and was now awakening from its winter sleep, drunken with water, bursting with the fresh rise of sap; throughout it rang the wild laughter of an exultant Spring which found an echo, a double, as it were, in my own heart. (p. 46)

nine). However, in Part Two, we witness the failure of this attempt to enjoy with the pregnant Marceline 'un uniforme bien-être où le soir s'unissait au matin, où les jours se liaient aux jours' (p. 81).[1] In the first chapter the movement of Part One is repeated. Marceline is gradually excluded as Michel becomes involved with Charles in the organization of his estates in La Morinière. We note a developing tension between 'l'éclatement fécond de la libre nature' and 'l'effort savant de l'homme pour la régler' (p. 82)[2] and not the perfect balance that Michel first perceives. By the end of this period, Michel, through contact with Charles and his agricultural ideas has been directed back to his interest in what he calls the 'rude, savage' culture of the Goths. That he was at the time only vaguely aware of the real direction of his behaviour is seen in the strange sense of unreality he feels in his love for Marceline (pp. 96–7).[3]

The central chapter of Part Two sees Michel drawn towards a rejection of civilized culture and social values under the influence of Ménalque. At the outset Michel is determined to commit himself once more to social life but in his extreme self-confidence, as Michel hints in his retrospective account, a dangerous tendency towards extravagance and self-delusion is apparent.

> A toutes ses craintes j'opposais une factice horreur du provisoire; je me forçais moi-même d'y croire et l'exagérais à dessein. Certainement les divers frais d'installation excéderaient nos revenus cette année, mais notre fortune déjà belle devait s'embellir encore; je comptais pour cela sur mon cours, sur la publication de mon livre et même, avec quelle folie! sur les nouveaux rendements de mes

[1] '. . . a state of changeless ease, in which evening joined morning without a break, in which day passed into day without a surprise.' (p. 70)

[2] '. . . the teeming fecundity of nature . . ., the wise effort of man to regulate it . . .' (p. 71)

[3] pp. 83–4.

fermes. Je ne m'arrêtais donc devant aucune dépense . . .
(p. 99)[1]

But the 'vagabond inclinations' which Michel tried to suppress
for the sake of Marceline and their unborn child are very soon
in evidence. He feels superior to his society friends in Paris,
resents that he is forced to play a social role and, because of his
intensely physical experience of death and life, feels isolated in
a world of shallow artificiality.

Four crucial meetings with an old friend, Ménalque, further
undermine Michel's attachment to his social and domestic
duties and lead him to develop a more systematically individualistic attitude. During the first and second (pp. 104–11)[2]
Ménalque comments on Michel's gradual shift towards individualism, seen in Part One, and proceeds to state the logical
consequences of this attitude, based on a hatred of possessions
and security, and on a love of travel and danger. He then
castigates Michel for what Michel himself had already been
partially aware of, the inconsistency between his present way of
life and his personal philosophy.

Ménalque's influence is immediately seen in Michel's dissatisfaction with his academic work (pp. 111–12) and in his
even stronger sense of disgust at the artificiality of Marceline's
soirées (pp. 112–13),[3] in contrast with his obvious attraction for
Ménalque's physical appearance, leading to his admiration
for Ménalque's systematic immoralism:

> Cette agoraphobie morale m'est odieuse; c'est la pire des

---

[1] I countered all her fears by pretending I had a horror of anything
temporary; I forced myself to believe in this feeling and deliberately
exaggerated it. Certainly the cost of furnishing and arranging the apart-
ment would exceed our income in the present year, but our fortune, which
was already large, was sure to increase still further; I counted on my
lectures for this, on the publication of my book and, such was my folly, on
the profits from my new farms. In consequence, I stopped short at no
expense . . . (p. 86)

[2] pp. 91–6.

[3] pp. 96–7, 97–8.

lâchetés. Pourtant c'est toujours seul qu'on invente. Mais qui cherche ici à inventer? Ce que l'on sent en soi de différent, c'est précisément ce que l'on possède de rare, ce qui fait à chacun sa valeur; et c'est là ce que l'on tâche de supprimer. On imite. Et l'on prétend aimer la vie. (p. 115)[1]

Michel's increasing interest in these ideas is symbolically connected with hints of Marceline's physical decline. Despite his concern at her health, he abandons her to spend the night with Ménalque and, after once again being subjected to individualistic propaganda, returns to find Marceline in the throes of a miscarriage.

During the debates with Ménalque, Michel, seeing the future in terms of his unborn son, just manages to hold off thoughts of breaking free. Loss of the child and Marceline's subsequent illness, however, provoke a situation parallel to that described in Part One, but where the roles are reversed. This is emphasized by Michel's irritation at Marceline's search for her rosary, recalling his rejection of her prayers during his own illness. His earlier hostility to the very idea of illness is revived and illustrated in his sudden lack of human sympathy for Marceline.

Cependant l'embolie avait amené des désordres assez graves; l'affreux caillot de sang, que le cœur avait rejeté, fatiguait et congestionnait les poumons, obstruait la respiration, la faisait difficile et sifflante. La maladie était entrée en Marceline, l'habitait désormais, la marquait, la tachait. C'était une chose abîmée. (pp. 126-7)[2]

---

[1] I detest such moral agoraphobia – the most obvious cowardice, I call it. Why, one always has to be alone to invent anything – but they don't want to invent anything. The part in each of us that we feel is different from other people is just the part that is rare, the part that makes our special value – and that is the very thing people try to suppress. They go on imitating. And yet they think that they love life. (p. 100)

[2] Meanwhile the horrible clot has brought on serious trouble; after her

Despite this traumatic insight, Michel still has the best of intentions towards Marceline. He wore himself out nursing her and wished to take her to convalesce in the mountains. But, for his sake, she insisted they return to La Morinière, encouraging him to 'courir sur les terres' (p. 129),[1] thus ironically promoting the relentless drive towards immoralism recorded in the remainder of the book. In the third chapter of Part Two Michel's rediscovery of the world of physical sensation is accompanied by his progressive alienation from the social conventions and responsibilities so scorned by Ménalque. Irritated by Marceline's visitors, he prefers the company of the farm-labourers with whom, in a voyeuristic manner, he identifies, seeking to enter into every aspect of their lives.

Gide underlines the shift in Michel's attitudes since the encounter with Ménalque by a repetition of certain key descriptions and events in Part Two, chapter one. Michel's awareness of Charles's naturalness as against Bocage's sententiousness and complacency (pp. 83–4)[2] is echoed in the contrast between Ménalque and the visitors to the Thursday *soirées*. Then, in chapter three, there is a striking reversal of roles as Michel becomes more anti-social: Charles is transformed into an absurdly conventional figure – an anti-Ménalque – driving Michel to prefer the skulking animality of Alcide, an echo of Moktir, the young Arab boy of Part One. In his defence of the drunken labourer, his association with Heurtevent and the woodcutters and, finally, in his active involvement with Bute and Alcide in poaching, Michel becomes increasingly identified with the forces of social dissolution. The result is the complete break-up of his estates after Charles, echoing

---

heart had escaped, it attacked her lungs, brought on congestion, impeded her breathing, made it short and laborious. Disease had taken hold of Marceline, never again to leave her; it had marked her, stained her. Henceforth she was a thing that had been spoiled. (p. 111)

[1] 'to visit the estate immediately'. (p. 112)
[2] pp. 72–3.

Ménalque, reproaches him for wanting to be 'à la fois le garde et le braconnier' (p. 148).[1]

Still, Michel attempts to live this double life and reconcile his love for Marceline with his impulse towards individual freedom. The problem, and it is one that Michel is brutally self-critical about in his retrospective account, is that his personal quest involves estrangement from Marceline, as Ménalque had so carefully pointed out. At the end of Part Two Marceline's illness and reproachful words produce in Michel sudden feelings of guilt and the desire to recapture the love they had shared at Sorrento. Part Three, faithful to Ménalque's prediction, vividly charts Michel's failure to harmonize the contradiction between duty to Marceline and duty to himself.

He acts the part of the loving husband for her sake and not out of any real need for a loving relationship. The relative positions of the couple are tellingly reversed. Every intoxicating contact with the physical world of sights and smells invigorates Michel and brings a deterioration in Marceline's health, as they retrace the steps of Michel's recuperation of Part One.

> Et de même que de semaine en semaine, lors de notre premier voyage, je marchais vers la guérison, de semaine en semaine, à mesure que nous avancions vers le Sud, l'état de Marceline empirait. (pp. 164–5)[2]

What is more, Michel's life becomes joyless and degrading. His renewed interest in the possibilities of human behaviour hidden by the thin veneer of culture, decency and morality leads him to leave Marceline for the company of social outcasts and criminals in the slums of various Italian cities, and this culminates in the night spent with the vermin-infested Arabs in

---

[1] 'both the keeper and the poacher at the same time'. (p. 130)

[2] And as during our first journey I had week by week progressed towards recovery, so week by week as we went southwards, Marceline's health grew worse. (p. 145)

Kairouan (p. 168).[1] Finally, Michel's abandonment of conventional moral values is graphically illustrated by the effect his own story has on him, momentarily pushing to the back of his mind all feelings of guilt and repentance.

> Assez longtemps j'ai cherché de vous dire comment je devins qui je suis. Ah! désembarrasser mon esprit de cette insupportable logique! . . . Je ne sens rien que de noble en moi. (p. 168)[2]

Not only is Marceline's health destroyed, then, but also, in reliving the days of his recuperation at Biskra, Michel finds everything debased. The Arab boys have lost their youthful innocence and Moktir is a convicted criminal. By now, however, Michel relentlessly pursues his individualistic quest, driven as if by some demon. In a striking passage Michel's thoughts of his earlier recovery at Biskra mingle suggestively with his concern at Marceline's health, ending with the triumph of Michel's self-interest. The rapid, staccato rhythm as impressions from past, present and an anticipated future crowd in on Michel, indicates a breakdown of linguistic order and control that mirrors Michel's moral state.

> Biskra. C'est donc là que je veux en venir. Oui; voici le jardin public; le banc . . . je reconnais le banc où je m'assis aux premiers jours de ma convalescence. Qu'y lisais-je donc? . . . Homère; depuis je ne l'ai pas rouvert. – Voici l'arbre dont j'allai palper l'écorce. Que j'étais faible, alors! . . . Tiens! voici des enfants . . . Non, je n'en reconnais aucun. Que Marceline est grave! Elle est aussi changée que moi. Pourquoi tousse-t-elle, par ce beau temps? – Voici l'hôtel. Voici nos chambres, nos terrasses. – Que pense Marceline? Elle ne m'a pas dit un mot. –

[1] p. 148.

[2] I have been long enough trying to explain how I became what I am. Oh, if only I could rid my mind of all this intolerable logic! . . . I feel I have nothing in me that is not noble. (p. 147)

Sitôt arrivée dans sa chambre, elle s'étend sur le lit; elle est lasse et dit vouloir dormir un peu. Je sors. (p. 169)[1]

The final outrage is when Michel enjoys Touggourt night-life with Moktir, sleeps with his mistress and returns home to find Marceline on her death-bed. The stark description of her final moments contains a complex mixture of horror, hostility and guilt; and when, echoing two previous scenes, Marceline rejects the crucifix, there is an awful sense of the triumph of evil over good.

Michel's attachment to life as an absolute has tragic consequences. It is all-consuming, destroying his wife and undermining his will power. It is this last effect that is stressed most strongly in the closing section of the book. Michel now lives like a prisoner in his isolated villa, fed by a sympathetic inn-keeper and dependent for company on a young Arab boy. The clarity and vigour of Michel's account, and the relentless movement towards a tragic climax, give way to a static, expressionless prose, indicating the ultimate debasement of Michel's ideal.

La Porte étroite

As with Michel in *L'Immoraliste* we can detect in Jérôme's account a desire for self-justification by means of a subconscious re-ordering of events that goes against his claim to reject any 'invention pour les rapiécer ou les joindre' (p. 5).[2] The effect of

---

[1] Biskra! That then was my goal ... Yes; there are the public gardens; the bench ... I recognize the bench on which I used to sit in the first days of my convalescence. What was it I read there? ... Homer; I have not opened the book since. There is the tree with the curious bark I got up to go and feel. How weak I was then! Look! there come some children! ... No; I recognize none of them. How grave Marceline is! She is as changed as I. Why does she cough so in this fine weather? There is the hotel! There are our rooms, our terrace! What is Marceline thinking? She has not said a word. As soon as she gets to her room she lies down on the bed; she is tired and says she wants to sleep a little. I go out. (p. 149)

[2] 'I shall have recourse to no invention, and neither patch nor connect them'. (p. 9)

Gide's use of a first-person narrative technique is in fact to make the reader both sympathetic and hostile to Jérôme: on the one hand, it enables the reader to focus critically on the gap between superficial appearances and underlying, often subconscious, factors in the behaviour of Jérôme and Alissa; but equally it helps to persuade the reader that their lack of self-knowledge and their possible self-deception are vital ingredients in the irreversible movement towards the tragic conclusion of the book.

Jérôme's restrained style is seen early in chapter one in the objective description of the Bucolin household (pp. 6–7),[1] coloured only in the final sentences by a muted lyricism. What becomes clear in the course of the chapter is that this passive tone is the literary reflection of a moral attitude – a life-denying Puritanism associated with his mother, with Flora Ashburton and notably with Alissa. Thus, despite Jérôme's obvious attraction for the exotic and beautiful outsider, Lucile Bucolin, there is an emphasis on her unseemly physical qualities ('ces corsages légers et largement ouverts . . . l'ardente couleur des écharpes que ma tante jetait sur ses épaules nues, ce décol-letage . . .')[2] and this is dramatically highlighted by Jérôme's sense of disgust at her playful sensuality (p. 13).[3] Later this point of view finds striking confirmation in Lucile's infidelity, wit-nessed by Jérôme; and it is fully articulated in the sermon at the end of the chapter.

What is also clear, however, is that Jérôme's hatred of Lucile Bucolin is inseparable from his attraction for Alissa, whose physical qualities are deliberately played down and who is presented in the highly dramatic bedroom scene as the pathetic victim of her mother's immorality. And just as Jérôme had identified Alissa imprecisely with different forms of ideal

[1] pp. 9–10.
[2] 'the transparent, low-necked bodices . . . the brilliant colour of the scarves which she used to throw over her bare shoulders, my aunt's low necks . . .' (p. 12)
[3] pp. 14–15.

beauty (p. 16),[1] so his love for her, which starts from a physical base, is dominated by a mixture of innocent and transcendental impulses:

> Je ne savais rien exprimer du transport nouveau de mon cœur; mais je pressais sa tête contre mon cœur et sur son front mes lèvres par où mon âme s'écoulait. Ivre d'amour, de pitié, d'un indistinct mélange d'enthousiasme, d'abnégation et de vertu, j'en appelais à Dieu de toutes mes forces et m'offrais, ne concevant plus d'autre but à ma vie que d'abriter cette enfant contre la peur, contre le mal, contre la vie. (pp. 19–20)[2]

Obsessed by Alissa and his mystical love for her, Jérôme underrates others like Abel Gautier and Robert Bucolin and this prepares the reader for the examination of Jérôme's treatment of Juliette in chapters two, three and four. Jérôme's possible blindness in this respect is already suggested in the confusion of Félicie Plantier who believes he loves Juliette (pp. 34–5)[3] and in Jérôme's complete insensitivity to the feelings of others seen in his insincere Romantic flight of fancy, wounding both to Juliette, who shares his assumed views, and to the eavesdropping Alissa, to whom Jérôme's words are in fact directed (pp. 39–47).[4]

Despite their apparent love for one another, Jérôme and Alissa are exceedingly inhibited in each other's company. In this, Jérôme's great timidity and fear of offending Alissa is a crucial factor, but Alissa's motives for the distance she places

---

[1] p. 16.

[2] I could express nothing of the unfamiliar transport of my breast, but I pressed her head against my heart, and I pressed my lips to her forehead, while my whole soul came flooding through them. Drunken with love, with piety, with an indistinguishable mixture of enthusiasm, of self-sacrifice, of virtue, I appealed to God with all my strength – I offered myself up to Him, unable to conceive that existence could have any other object than to shelter this child from fear, from evil, from life. (p. 19)

[3] pp. 29–30.

[4] pp. 32–7.

between them are noticeably veiled. The contrast between the calm serenity of Jérôme's feelings for Alissa and Abel's exultant Romantic enthusiasm for Juliette leads on to a new view of Juliette as the victim of Alissa and Jérôme and to a suggestion of their combined egoism. But this is only half the truth, as Abel and Jérôme discover at the end of chapter four, when certain vital facts emerge to explain Juliette's hesitation to marry her suitor and Alissa's ambiguous attitude to Jérôme, as well as to underline Jérôme's chronic lack of perception.

Three *coups de théâtre* follow in rapid succession: we learn that Alissa wants Jérôme to marry Juliette; Abel then reveals that this is because Alissa knows that Juliette loves Jérôme; finally, in response to Alissa's sacrifice, Juliette hurriedly agrees to marry her suitor, Tessières, and at a moment of high tension she faints. In this very dramatic scene at the end of chapter four, Jérôme's incomprehension, Abel's helpless anger and Alissa's despair are juxtaposed as Juliette makes her sacrifice. And Jérôme, rooted to the spot, witnesses from a distance the symbolic gathering of interested parties around Juliette's inert body:

> Ma tante et le prétendant maintiennent Juliette sous les épaules, à demi renversée dans leurs bras. Alissa soulève les pieds de sa sœur et les embrasse tendrement. Abel soutient la tête qui retomberait en arrière, – et je le vois courbé, couvrir de baisers ces cheveux abandonnés qu'il rassemble. (p. 80)[1]

To the end Jérôme remains unaware of his own responsibility in this complex chain of events.

The presentation of Jérôme as an outsider is reinforced by

[1] My aunt and the stranger [*sic*] were supporting Juliette's shoulders, as she lay, half reclining in their arms. Alissa raised her sister's feet and embraced them tenderly. Abel held up her head, which would have fallen backwards, and I saw him bend down and cover with kisses her floating hair, as he gathered it together. (p. 61)

his geographical estrangement from the Bucolin household in chapter five. He is dependent for news on Robert, Félicie Plantier, and Alissa, who insists that he stays away. From a distance he witnesses Juliette's obstinate self-sacrifice and her courageous acceptance of her new family duties, eventually gaining Alissa's approval. He also has to undergo Alissa's diagnosis of the situation.

For, in order to guarantee contact with Alissa, Jérôme has to forgo talk of marriage and becomes trapped in a platonic relationship. He notes passages in his reading in which he believes she will be interested and she seems to take this as evidence that he shares her sense of religious duty. We see her fighting to suppress her desire to be near him and seeking everywhere for arguments to justify this action. Obsessed with her duty to God and with the idea that it is irreconcilable with earthly happiness, she is born along on the wave of poetic mysticism. In this way her capacity for emotion and physical involvement is directed away from Jérôme towards God: even her contact with the world of sensation has all the accents of otherworldly requirements.

> 'L'hymne confus' de la nature. Je l'entends dans chaque chant d'oiseau: je la respire dans le parfum de chaque fleur, et j'en viens à ne comprendre plus que l'adoration comme seule forme de la prière. (p. 96)[1]

Thus, all things are subordinate to the need to prepare for salvation, and to that end Jérôme must not tempt her with the possibility of earthly happiness. In one way, we see Jérôme as the victim of Alissa's rejection of life, just as Juliette was rejected by Jérôme because of his attachment to the spiritual values represented by Alissa. On the other hand, we hesitate

---

[1] Nature's 'mingled hymn'. I hear it in every bird's song; I breathe it in the scent of every flower, and I have reached the point of conceiving adoration as the only form of prayer. (p. 70)

to condemn Alissa for her somewhat harsh treatment of Jérôme because her struggle to do what she believes to be right for her and Jérôme causes her so much pain. Still, however, the ambiguity remains: do her letters simply illustrate the tragic struggle between love to Jérôme and duty to God, or are they not equally a cruel reminder to Jérôme that this duty is self-imposed and that their love can only be maintained at a distance?

In the long drawn-out central section of the book running from Lucile Bucolin's elopement to the death of Alissa there is, despite the superficial predominance of Jérôme's point of view, a gradual shift of attention from Jérôme to Juliette, back to Jérôme and on to Alissa. As we have seen, in chapters two to four Alissa's otherworldly aspirations and readiness to sacrifice Jérôme's love in favour of Juliette are thwarted by Jérôme's persistent love for Alissa and by Juliette's equal determination to sacrifice her love for Jérôme. The pathos of Juliette's sacrifice, dramatically emphasized at the end of chapter four is driven home by references in chapter five to her heroic acceptance of her duties to family life.

In chapters five to eight the focus is on Jérôme as the victim of Alissa's mystical urge. He accepts her view of their relationship, partly because he shares it to a degree and partly because he believes that they will eventually be united. And whereas Alissa appears perverse in her desire to turn away from Jérôme and life, Jérôme finds it clearly impossible to suppress his natural feelings for her:

'Alissa! qui donc épouserai-je? Tu sais pourtant que je ne puis aimer que toi ... ' et tout à coup, la serrant éperdument presque brutalement dans mes bras, j'écrasais de baisers ses lèvres. Un instant comme abandonnée je la tins à demi renversée. contre moi; je vis son regard se voiler; puis ses paupières se fermèrent, et d'une voix dont rien n'égalera pour moi la justesse et la mélodie:

'Aie pitié de nous, mon ami! Ah! n'abîme pas notre amour.' (p. 144)[1]

At no point in the book do Jérôme and Alissa seem further apart in their expectation of love and life. And yet, here Alissa emerges as much the victim of Jérôme's insensitivity as Juliette had in chapter four. For, Jérôme, as an interested party, has been less than aware of Alissa's pathetic struggle to suppress her love, and the many hints of emotional complexity that the discerning reader might have noted in her letters find striking confirmation later in her Diary. In it the full extent of Alissa's tragedy is outlined. From the fictional point of view it is the precise complement of Jérôme's account which is slightly disjointed and ambiguous. On one level, therefore, we note the discrepancy between the two accounts, suggesting Jérôme's weakness and confusion as well as confirming Alissa's systematic attempt to suppress her love for Jérôme. But, looking more closely, we become aware, ironically, that she finds herself in a tragic *impasse*. Not only was her exaggerated piety a measure of the great love she continued to feel for Jérôme, but also, in sacrificing it for the sake of her spiritual salvation, she discovers that without it her very salvation is in fact at risk.

Consequently, the reader becomes aware of the enormous gap between her uncompromising ideals and the final impression of her as a frail, uncertain and all too human figure. At the end, Alissa recognizes the distance between her ideal of happiness in God and the mental suffering that this has actually involved.

Il s'est d'abord fait dans tout mon être un grand calme; puis une angoisse s'est emparée de moi, un frisson de la

---

[1] 'Alissa! whom should I marry? You know I can love no one but you . . .' and suddenly clasping her wildly, almost brutally in my arms, I crushed my kisses on her lips. An instant I held her unresisting, as she half lay back against me; I saw her look grow dim; then her eyes closed, and in a voice so true and melodious that never to my mind will it be equalled; 'Have pity on us, my friend!' she said. 'Oh! don't spoil our love.' (p. 103)

chair et de l'âme, c'était comme l'*éclaircissement* brusque et désenchanté de ma vie. Il me semblait que je voyais pour la première fois les murs atrocement nus de ma chambre . . . Je voudrais mourir à présent, vite, avant d'avoir compris de nouveau que je suis seule. (p. 173)[1]

In *La Porte étroite* there is, until the final revelations of Alissa's Diary, a superficial impression of diversity and disjointedness which mirrors Jérôme's constant feeling of puzzlement. But this apparent artlessness in the narrative technique is soon belied by the cumulative effect of symbolic descriptions (the garden at Fongueusemare), recurrent scenes (Alissa's bedroom) and symbols (doors, gates, paths), all defined in terms of a basic dichotomy between the values of a puritanical faith and those connected with life and human experience. In addition, characters are grouped in relation to this basic conflict. One group of characters consistently turn their backs on life – Jérôme's mother, Alissa's father and pastor Vautier – and they are set against Lucile Bucolin, Félicie Plantier and Abel Vautier. In the middle are three characters – Jérôme, Alissa and Juliette – whose lives are destroyed, because of their interlocking destinies, by these irreconcilable values. The sense of fatality is on one occasion underpinned by the parallel between Alissa's father, Félicie Plantier and Jérôme's mother in their youth, and Jérôme, Juliette and Alissa. Also, in the contrast between Alissa and Lucile Bucolin it becomes clear how one extreme of behaviour provokes another. Alissa systematically suppresses all that Lucile represents but, in the process, discovers both the force and the attraction of human nature in herself. Jérôme, too, initially suppresses his instinctive admiration for Lucile's physical qualities, only to become

---

[1] First a great calm fell upon my whole being; then a pang of anguish pierced me, a shudder of my flesh and soul; it was like the sudden and disenchanting *illumination* of my life. It seemed to me that I saw for the first time the walls of my room in their atrocious bareness. . . . I should like to die now, quickly, before again realizing that I am alone. (p. 125)

identified with physical demands in contrast to Alissa's extreme spirituality. Underlying the whole tragedy of the relationship between Jérôme and Alissa is the brilliantly suggested tragedy of Juliette. Her unrequited love for Jérôme and her sacrifice of it in her marriage to Tessières are movingly recalled in the closing lines of the book, as Jérôme's mixture of awe and admiration for Alissa's sacrifice reminds her brutally of her own, underlining the sense of tragic waste that Jérôme has experienced with Alissa.

3

Les Caves du Vatican

(i) *Humour and Irony*

Les Caves du Vatican was first presented to the public as a 'sotie, par l'auteur de *Paludes*'. With this sub-title Gide connects his new work with the finely-wrought ironical structure of *Paludes* and the burlesque and inconsequential humour of *Le Prométhée mal enchaîné*, which he published more than a decade earlier. The use of the term *sotie* also places this new work in a comic tradition that goes back to the popular satirical plays of the late-medieval theatre and beyond this to the traditional carnival rites associated with the major church festivals such as Christmas and Easter. In the *soties* the actors all wore fools' costumes and, with a combination of grotesque clowning and vigorous popular humour, ridiculed leading local or national dignitaries.

Gide's book bears many traces of this satirical manner. His puppet-like characters are all extreme parodies of certain social types – the Freemason/scientist, the aristocratic Catholic novelist, the arch-criminal and the pious believer. Gide emphasizes the contrast between them in their dress, their speech and their characteristic attachment to their own view of reality. Anthime's bluntness and cynicism contrast Julius's pomposity and complacency. There is another extreme contrast between the quick-wittedness of the villain, Protos, and the extreme gullibility of the would-be knight-errant, Amédée Fleurissoire. Their very names are a comic and, sometimes, satirical comment on their behaviour. Anthime Armand-Dubois combines the name of an early Eastern saint with a

suggestion of his need to use a crutch (en s'armant du bois).
Baraglioul may owe something to the name de Broglie, the
monarchist diplomat and writer, and to two words, *baragouiner*
(to jabber, talk nonsense) and *barbouilleur* (second-rate artist,
scribbler). Amédée suggests an important spiritual vocation
and his surname Fleurissoire (*fleurir*, to blossom, flourish)
is an ironic comment on this sickly plant which, when up-
rooted from its natural environment, is manipulated by Protos
and deflowered by a prostitute aptly named Venitequa (Italian
= come hither). Protos's name suggests his Protean ability to
change his appearance, while the crude prediction in Philibert
Péterat (*péter*, to fart) is thrown into relief by the botanical
names of his daughters, Marguerite, Véronique and Arnica,
and his servant, Réséda. This verbal humour is found also in
the name Blafaphas (*blafard* + *face*), with its various spellings,
the joint surname, les Blafafoires, and the doubly Jewish name
Lévichon (Lévy + Cohen).

To this should be added Gide's use of puns, rare and technical terms, his introduction of quotations from Italian and
English and his exploitation of a whole range of syntactical
phenomena, combining popular forms with archaic or hyper-
correct constructions. At the same time, Gide's tendency to
link his characters with bizarre and often unexpected objects
gives rise to some noteworthy comic imagery, involving the
exaggeration of certain physical or psychological traits. Thus,
the whimsical description of Carola as 'une fleur azurée au
milieu d'un tas de fumier' (p. 143),[1] the association of Amédée's
boater with the bobbing action of a valve, or the rigidity of his
starched collar compared with the slender, worm-like necktie
worn by Lafcadio, all contribute to Gide's attempt at an absurd,
baroque style appropriate for this comic novel.

Much of the comedy derives from the clash of two opposing
characters each mechanically acting out his role in situations
that frequently border on farce. The brilliantly orchestrated

[1] 'just as an azure-tinted flower . . . in the middle of a dung-heap'. (p. 134)

scene in which Protos, disguised as a priest, attempts to dupe the pious comtesse de Saint-Prix (pp. 93–107)[1] reveals the materialism of the victim, which is overcome only by Protos's highly emotional and dramatic performance as a Catholic secret agent. Equally burlesque is the episode in which Protos and the false cardinal, Bardolotti, persuade Amédée, in the midst of an orgy of wine, food and women, of the high seriousness of their mission to rescue the Pope and ritually absolve Amédée of his adultery with Carola. Such theatrical moments, together with repeated dialogues and debates between successive pairs of characters, emphasize the hybrid quality of *Les Caves du Vatican* which is in every way an experimental novel.

In this critical work Gide employs a whole set of ironical procedures. The apparently open structure provides for a number of parallels, by which the behaviour of the major characters can be compared and contrasted. By a process of duplication and even multiplication, key ideas are progressively devalued. Julius's excitement at his discovery in Book Four of new psychological theories is repeated in Lafcadio's intense fascination at his own powers before the murder and this is parodied in Defoulqueblize's intoxication as he restates the same ideas. To emphasize the connexion, Julius's later words ('nous vivons contrefaits', p. 204)[2] are echoed by Defoulqueblize ('des gens de la société . . . se doivent de vivre contrefaits', p. 225),[3] and his 'quel avantage pour le bâtard' (p. 226)[4] restates Juste-Agénor's 'vous ne serez jamais qu'un bâtard' (p. 70).[5] It is even possible to detect verbal and structural connexions between complete scenes, as in the three 'bedroom' incidents in which Anthime, Amédée and Lafcadio each receive a female visitor: a ghostly figure at first re-

[1] pp. 85–98.
[2] 'we prefer to go deformed and distorted all our lives'. (p. 193)
[3] 'people who are in society . . . owe it to ourselves to go masked.' (p. 214)
[4] 'what an advantage for the bastard'. (p. 215)
[5] 'you will never be anything but a bastard'. (p. 64)

sembling Julie, the prostitute, Carola, and Geneviève de
Baraglioul.

Irony involves also the manipulation of language to suggest
meanings in direct opposition to those apparent on the surface.
Some obvious examples are the 'manière de concorde' and 'sorte
de demi-félicité' of Anthime and Véronique and the master-
piece of understatement concerning the narrowness of Julius's
experience of life:

> Malgré certaine curiosité professionnelle et la flatteuse
> illusion que rien d'humain ne lui devait demeurer étranger,
> Julius était peu descendu jusqu'à présent hors des cou-
> tumes de sa classe et n'avait guère eu de rapports qu'avec
> des gens de son milieu. L'occasion, plutôt que le goût, lui
> manquait. (p. 49)[1]

Here the language is formal, inflated and academic, used in a
casuistical way, as if it were a piece of special pleading by
Julius. Wrapped in verbiage, a self-evident weakness poses as
a sort of virtue. It works in rather the same way as when Gide
places in his characters' mouths words that assume attitudes
totally out of character. One thinks of Amédée's heroic self-
sacrifice at hearing the news of the Pope's imprisonment, and
the formal admonitions of Lafcadio to Geneviève in the final
scene of the novel.

Ironical procedures of this kind abound in this richly comic
novel. Nothing is taken at its face value: individual interpretations of reality are shown to be inadequate. Rigid commitment to any absolute truth, such as that represented by the
Vatican, can make *caves* or dupes of us all.

---

[1] Notwithstanding a certain amount of professional curiosity and the
flattering illusion that nothing human was alien to him, Julius had rarely
derogated from the customs of his class and he had very few dealings
except with persons of his own *milieu*. This was from lack of opportunity
rather than of taste. (p. 44)

(ii) *A Novel Procedure*

Les Caves du Vatican was Gide's first conscious and serious attempt to advance significantly beyond the outdated nineteenth-century theories of Realism and Naturalism. In the novel, he felt, it should be possible to express the pulse and richness of life. Where Balzac and his heirs fell down, for all their achievements, was in their assumption that there was one universally held view of reality. Characters were arbitrarily situated in a recognizable world that was real only in the most superficial sense. By its very rationality, this external reality seemed to deny the existence of deeper and more complex aspects of reality, based on subjective experience.

Gide's approach to the problem can be seen on two main levels in *Les Caves du Vatican*. In the first place, he presents a criticism of the traditional novel through his second-rate novelist, Julius de Baraglioul, whose theories are illustrated in his unsuccessful novel, *L'Air des Cimes*, as well as in Gide's own parody for comic purposes of many of the conventional procedures. Julius's novel, based on the career of his own father, is criticized by all but the most inane of reviewers because it presents a colourless imitation of real life. It lacks credibility because of Julius's oversimplified view of human nature, and for Lafcadio it is a grotesquely inadequate image of the man of flesh and blood he meets in the course of Book Two. As an alternative Lafcadio himself is the kind of unpredictable and complex character that it is the novelist's duty to portray. During the course of the final book of *Les Caves du Vatican*, Julius is momentarily drawn by such a hero, but ironically he reverts to his conventional position when reports of Amédée's murder confirm that his fascinating hypothesis exists in 'real life'.

Anthime in Book One and Amédée in Book Three are absurd examples of the rigid determinism of character Gide deplores in the late nineteenth-century novel. Anthime's behaviour and attitudes are determined by his physical disability and they in turn condition his relationship with his wife and family. Because of the information the reader is given early in the novel, Anthime's actions are mechanical and predictable. In a similar way, Amédée's reactions in Book Four can be narrowly attributed to social and psychological factors outlined in the second half of Book Three. As a complete contrast, Lafcadio's inconsequential behaviour in Book Two remains a mystery to the reader until the partial explanations given by Lafcadio himself when he describes his upbringing to Julius.

Gide also calls into question the logic and order of the traditional plot. The five-part structure of *Les Caves du Vatican* is a deliberate attempt to open out the conventional novel form so that it can become a meeting-place for conflicting points of view. As the centre of interest shifts radically from Anthime to Julius and Lafcadio, and on to Protos and Amédée Fleurissoire, an impression of disjointedness is produced. This is further encouraged by the various interruptions and digressions made by the author. Anthime's wen, the discussion of Lafcadio's 'banal' love affair with Geneviève, Amédée's comic encounter with bed-bugs and mosquitoes, the bizarre relationship between him and Carola – all these are felt by the reader to be interruptions in the narrative flow. In addition, each of the major characters is involved in a different drama and it is only the action of Protos that effectively brings them together in Rome. He is the fictional reflection of the author, whose job it is to set out the conditions of the artistic experience. It is for the reader, on the other hand, to pull together the threads in a process of active collaboration with the author. The idea seems to be to create an illusion of chaos and, in doing so, bring the reader face to face with the strangeness and complexity of life, presented in terms of farce.

The fantasy world which Gide presents in *Les Caves du Vatican* is a distorted picture of real life. The action is set in a precise historical and social context. Protos's scheme, however fantastic it might seem, actually occurred in Lyons in the

1890s. Anthime's conversion was no more unlikely than those of Zola's Freemason cousin and the many dramatic conversions of Naturalist writers like Bourget and Huysmans. The curious mixture of fantasy and reality that gives *Les Caves du Vatican* its comic and satirical power can be best illustrated in the story Protos invents to dupe the comtesse de Saint-Prix. In it a whole number of historical facts and rumours are linked together in a logical sequence that make it plausible and rational in the mind of the countess because she is looking for an explanation for the Pope's surprising decision to call on French monarchists to rally to the Third Republic. Protos's richly comic performance as a Catholic priest – comic because the reader knows it to be fraudulent – exposes the partiality of the countess's viewpoint, and proposes the existence of a more complex set of circumstances, to which all those with limited vision are denied access.

In a similar way, all the characters who judge reality in the light of narrow preconceptions illustrate the danger of mistaking appearance for reality. All seem to respond, like crustaceans, in an instinctive and oversimplified way to life. Despite this, however, Gide manages to give them recognizable human shape at different moments in the book. Anthime and Julius, in particular, are seen in Books One and Two in sufficient psychological depth to be, potentially at least, rounded human characters. Even Amédée Fleurissoire is occasionally capable of inspiring sympathy for his agonizing inadequacies.

Les Caves du Vatican is more than just a comic novel with satirical overtones. It is a sort of hydra-headed literary monster, composed of elements drawn from many different types of novel, ranging from the eighteenth-century picaresque novel through Balzac, Dickens and Stevenson to the underworld thrillers popular at the turn of the century. The text is full of allusions to other works of fiction. Lafcadio recalls Fielding's Tom Jones, Stendhal's Julien Sorel, Balzac's Rastignac, Dostoevsky's Raskolnikov and many others. Gide even goes as far as to base episodes on the reconstruction of similar episodes from other books. Thus, Lafcadio's rescue of the children from the fire (pp. 64–6)[1] recalls a chapter from Lesage's *Diable boiteux* as well as Pierre's rescue of the young girl in Tolstoy's *War and Peace*. By using this technique and by making discreet allusions to his own earlier works Gide emphasizes the artificial, literary nature of his novel, deliberately distancing it from life.

This does not prevent the reader from experiencing an honest illusion of life. He may frequently be discomforted as he tries his keep up with an author who delights in conjuring up confusing situations and laying false trails. Yet, in attuning his wits to the task of relating apparently disparate elements to an artistic whole, he is brought into contact with the equivocal nature of reality itself. Thus, what might at first seem incredible and unreal, is in fact a brilliantly constructed working model of real life.

(iii) *Form and Development*

In planning his first large-scale novel Gide set out to juxtapose a number of different points of view, corresponding to the different characters involved. If the combination of these produces a sense of the relative complexity of human life, it does so only because of Gide's skilful manipulation of artistic elements and the imposition of formal control. The division of *Les Caves du Vatican* into five Books and the number of parts in each Book (7, 7, 4, 7, 7) is thus major confirmation of this concern for balance and symmetry.

Book One deals with the conversion in Rome of an intractable Freemason and scientist to the Catholic faith of his wife and family. There is a relentless predictability about the way in which the miracle-cure in Part VI fulfils their pious hopes. Despite repeated gestures in Parts II, III, IV and V to maintain his independence of mind and behaviour, Anthime returns to

[1] pp. 58–60.

physical and spiritual health. His new involvement in family
life owes much to his failure to endure his self-imposed isolation. There is a violent swing from Anthime, the grotesquely
maimed vivisectionist, seen through the eyes of his pious wife,
to the pliant convert of Part VII who has to endure public
display and material ruin as the price for his return to the fold.
In fact, he exchanges one fixed identity for another. By the
end of this Book the major themes of the novel are already
outlined. We note the failure to maintain his freedom in the
face of family pressures, the controlling self-interest of Anthime
and Julius, whose financial and professional success are linked
to their Freemasonry and Catholicism respectively, and, in the
burlesque parody of a miracle-cure, Gide's ironical comment
on the possible confusion between appearance and reality.

In Book Two the scene shifts to Paris, where the Baraglioul
family is about to be invaded by the enigmatic bastard son,
Lafcadio Wluiki. Here there is a careful structuring of events
around the central recognition scene between Juste-Agénor
and Lafcadio with its emphasis on the family as a closed society,
able to acknowledge 'natural' sons only in an underhand way.
Each side of this dramatic encounter are placed the two
meetings between Lafcadio and Geneviève (pp. 64–6, 75–7)[1]
and, encircling them, the two clashes between Lafcadio and
Julius (pp. 57–9, 77–95).[2] The shortcomings of Julius's new
novel in the opinion of Juste-Agénor and the critics are
echoed near the end by Lafcadio, and the introduction to
Lafcadio in Juste-Agénor's letter is balanced by Lafcadio's
departure from Paris at the end. Although ostensibly devoted
to Julius, the Book is dominated by Lafcadio, who has his
conformist half-brother constantly at a disadvantage. In fact,
they represent the negative and positive sides of Juste-Agénor's
personality.

The themes of self-interest and hypocrisy that inform Book
Two reach a comic climax in the reactions of the comtesse de

[1] pp. 58–60, 68–71. [2] pp. 51–3, 70–83.

Saint-Prix, whose name symbolizes the tension in her nature between materialism and piety. Her reactions find an echo in those of the Fleurissoires who, for all their absurd piety, had 'grande pudeur à l'endroit du porte-monnaie' (p. 116)[1]. The Fleurissoires are a distorted provincial reflection of the Baraglio#uls of Books One and Two. Indeed, a number of parallels and contrasts can be made: between the Fleurissoire/Blafaphas relationship and that of Protos and Lafcadio; between Amédée's unconsummated marriage and Julius's distance from Marguerite, as well as the coolness that exists between the Armand-Dubois; between the pathetic inadequacy of Amédée and the mental and physical prowess of Lafcadio (remembering that at the end of Part Three Amédée, like Lafcadio before him, is embarking on a journey).

The main characters are, by their own separate ways, being assembled in Italy ('Le jour même que Fleurissoire quittait Pau, Julius sonnait à la porte d'Anthime', p. 122).[2] In this final section of Book Three the positions of Julius, Anthime and Amédée are closely linked. Anthime's exaggerated piety echoes that of the Fleurissoires and contrasts the new cynicism of Julius and Véronique, a comic reversal of the roles played out in Book One.

In Book Four a burlesque climax is reached with Amédée's chequered progress towards Rome, his being conned by Baptistin, who finds him lodgings in a brothel, and his subsequent bewilderment in the company of Protos. On each return to his lodgings we note the growth of Carola's concern for Amédée, which at this stage seems bizarre and gratuitous. In the final part, Julius's meeting with Amédée parallels his visit to the Armand-Dubois in Book Three. We now see Julius envisaging a break with his past, just like Anthime, Lafcadio and Amédée before him.

[1] '[were] modestly shy of talking about their money matters'. (p. 107)
[2] 'On the same day that Fleurissoire left Pau, Julius knocked at Anthime's door'. (p. 113)

All of the characters are brought together in Book Five. Lafcadio is full of self-confidence and the desire to illustrate his complete freedom by committing an inexplicable, motiveless murder. He meets his victim, Amédée, only to discover, ironically, that not only was the act itself more difficult than he had imagined, but that also Amédée is a *carrefour*, a link with the past which he believed he had left behind. The crime has repercussions on each of the major characters, who give it a different significance. Julius sees it first as confirmation of his new psychological theories and then, remembering Amédée's confused story, becomes convinced that it was the work of the Pope's enemies. Lafcadio's initial sense of pride suffers when he witnesses this conclusion of Julius's and when he finds that Protos, who was keeping watch over Amédée all the time, tries to blackmail him into joining his gang. In addition, Carola believes Protos to be the murderer and denounces him to the police. Consequently Protos strangles her, is caught *in flagrante delicto* and found to have in his possession the incriminating evidence with which he had been hoping to blackmail Lafcadio.

Curiously, Lafcadio now feels an even greater sense of responsibility and guilt, and wishes to give himself up. Julius characteristically advises him to forget the whole thing, as does Geneviève. But Lafcadio's spirits are revived by Geneviève's visit to his bed, after which he seems to be hesitating between confession to the police and the possibility of moving to pastures new. As a result of Amédée's murder, Julius returns from the brink of revolt to his previous position, Anthime becomes once again a crippled atheist and Lafcadio, after a momentary loss of self-confidence, seems ready again to face up to the challenge of living.

(iv) *Lafcadio and the Quest for Authentic Behaviour*

Les Caves du Vatican is a literary and psychological experiment. Julius's 'new' hero, who closely resembles Lafcadio, has implications in real life, involving a challenge to over-simplified psychological explanations in terms of good and evil. All the conventionally good characters are subject to self-interest, pride and vanity – qualities they share, Gide points out, with conventional criminals like Protos. The moral bankruptcy of bourgeois society, symbolized by the Baraglioul family and its ramifications, involves also the stifling of natural impulses. On the margin of society, however, there is an assortment of characters – Beppo, Carola, Lafcadio and his 'uncles' – whose behaviour is considerably more sincere. That is to say, contradictory impulses in their natures find freer expression. For example, as an answer to the failure of conventional marriage, Gide hints at the sexual fulfilment of Lafcadio's mother, the humanity of Carola, the incestuous love of Lafcadio for Geneviève and the suggestions of homosexuality that attend every relationship Lafcadio has with an older man.

Conventional attitudes and judgements are inadequate responses to the complexity of real life. Society is full of 'crustaceans' against which are set the more flexible *subtils*. Broadly speaking, *subtils* value their moral freedom and are equipped to live according to the changing needs of their personalities, untrammelled by the dictates of social convention and family pressure. Their reflexes are quick and sophisticated, whereas those of the 'crustaceans' are rudimentary and predictable. The revolts of Anthime, Julius and Amédée against their early attitudes might seem by their very violence to be unpredictable, but the brothers-in-law are in fact the mindless victims of social forces, indoctrination and, in the case of Amédée, untruths. And Protos, it is true, has many of the attributes of the *subtils* but, for all his ability to manipulate his witless victims, he is in a fixed relationship to established society, one based on material gain. If Lafcadio's behaviour in Book Two owes something to a philosophy of life borrowed from Protos, he nevertheless finds his natural impulses constantly breaking through, as the episode of the self-inflicted wounds and the reactions to Geneviève and Juste-Agénor only serve to emphasize.

Lafcadio's true mentors are the successive lovers of his courtesan mother. Given the name of 'uncles', they form an anti-family, providing for the growing boy an education in the school of life. Lafcadio has an enjoyable and thoroughly practical grounding in basic skills – mathematics, four or five foreign languages and physical sports. With Baldi his sense of curiosity and fantasy was developed. From Faby he learned the pleasures of nudism and from Gesvres the art of fine clothes and a complete disregard for his financial interest. There is, throughout this description of his upbringing, an emphasis on naturalness, breadth and enjoyment without thought of profit. His bastardy, like that of many picaresque heroes, sets him outside family influence, without obligation or duty to others. Indeed, his behaviour and philosophy of life offers contrasts on every level with Anthime, Julius and, later, Amédée.

The fascination of 'crustaceans' for his freedom and *inconséquence* is seen in Julius's adoption of an equivalent fictional hero in Books Four and Five, and in the ravings of the 'arch-crustacean', Defoulqueblize, in Book Five. Of course, Lafcadio in Book Two is only *relatively* freer than the other characters in this comic novel. While pretending that his hero is getting out of hand, Gide is paradoxically assigning him the same fictional status as his other puppet-like heroes. Lafcadio's versatility is exaggerated and even, in the case of the attraction for Geneviève, mocked as being a conventional romantic cliché. Nevertheless, he does display a greater range of human reactions, a greater potential for coping with unexpected events. His contradictory behaviour is evidence of greater psychological depth that can be deduced from the actions of the other characters.

Seen in this light, his much discussed 'acte gratuit', the wilful murder of Amédée, might be seen as the logical extension

of his amoral attitude to life, whereby Gide tests in extreme
circumstances the consequences of a commitment to moral
freedom. Just before the murder the superhuman qualities of
Lafcadio are exaggerated. He is described at the peak of his
powers, anxious to give expression to his complex nature. He
has an acute sense of all the possibilities life has to offer:

> Mais la curiosité, c'est de savoir ce que la vieille aurait dit
> si j'avais commencé de serrer . . . On imagine *ce qui arriver-*
> *ait si*, mais il reste toujours un petit laps par où l'imprévu
> se fait jour. Rien ne se passe jamais tout à fait comme on
> aurait cru . . . C'est là ce qui me porte à agir . . . On fait
> si peu! . . . 'Que tout ce qui peut être soit!' c'est comme
> ça que je m'explique la Création . . . Amoureux de ce qui
> pourrait être . . . Si j'étais l'État, je me ferais enfermer.
> (p. 187)[1]

Locked in to the inexorable logic of his mental processes,
Lafcadio clearly overreaches himself. He becomes the victim
of his own curiosity and is so aloof from conventional moral
scruples that he grossly underrates the intellectual possibilities
of others.

> Belle collection de marionnettes; mais les fils sont trop
> apparents, par ma foi! On ne croise plus dans les rues que
> jean-foutres et paltoquets. Est-ce le fait d'un honnête
> homme, Lafcadio, je vous le demande, de prendre cette
> farce au sérieux? (p. 188)[2]

[1] But the curious thing would be to know what the old woman would
have said if I had begun to squeeze. One imagines *what would happen if*,
but there's always a little hiatus through which the unexpected creeps in.
Nothing ever happens exactly as one thinks it's going to. . . . That's what
makes me want to act. . . . One does so little! . . . 'Let all that can be, be!'
That's my explanation of the Creation. . . . In love with what might be. If
I were the Government I should lock myself up. (pp. 177–8)

[2] A fine lot of puppets; but, by Jove, one sees the strings too plainly.
One meets no one in the streets nowadays but jackanapes and blockheads.
Is it possible for a decent person – I ask you, Lafcadio – to take such a farce
seriously? (p. 178)

Lafcadio's blind arrogance here is apparent from the moment Amédée enters the compartment and Lafcadio confidently asserts: 'Entre ce sale magot et moi, quoi de commun?'[1] He later repeats the same fault in the encounter with Defoulque-blize, during which the reader is made to share with Lafcadio the shock of discovering that it is Protos in disguise.

During the final book the gap between the 'crustaceans' and Lafcadio is narrowed. Before the murder he displays much of Julius's smugness and complacency and his childish anarchism recalls Anthime's anti-social behaviour. And when Protos reveals his knowledge of the murder, Lafcadio, in a typically 'bourgeois' reaction, attempts to buy back from him the incriminating piece of leather cut from his hat. In the last five pages of the novel, this deflationary process is carried still further. Apparently wounded by Julius's failure to give him human contact and consolation, Lafcadio displays reactions that precisely echo those of the 'crustaceans'. His sense of abandonment and 'torpeur' recall those of Anthime (pp. 34, 36);[2] his application of the wet handkerchief to his heart and his formal speech to Geneviève both echo the behaviour of Julius in the preceding scene; finally his exaggerated sense of guilt and self-pity ('Je ne suis plus libre et plus digne de vous aimer', p. 247)[3] recall the earlier words of Amédée Fleurissoire to Bardolotti ('Je ne suis plus digne! Je ne suis plus digne!' etc., p. 166).[4]

With great subtlety, however, Gide sketches Lafcadio's awakening from this despondency. On the surface of the narrative it seems possible that Lafcadio, lured by the beautiful Geneviève, will give himself up to the police and Gide alludes to this in the final sentence of the book. This is, in fact, only an illusion. For, up to the moment that Lafcadio yields to his

[1] 'What is there in common between me and that squalid little rat?' (p. 179)
[2] pp. 30, 33.
[3] 'I am no longer free and no longer worthy to love you'. (p. 234)
[4] 'I'm no longer worthy! I'm no longer worthy!' (p. 155)

physical desire for Geneviève, he has been playing out a conventional moral role and his language has, as we have already noted, a self-conscious theatrical sound, reminiscent of Julius. Against this is set his increasing awareness of Geneviève's sexuality, which he briefly resists. The role of physical experience in revitalizing Lafcadio and liberating him from reactions and statements that connect him with the 'crustaceans' is strongly suggested in his thoughts after the love-making. Then, despite a tantalizing ambiguity, there is a definite feeling of renewal. Lafcadio, it seems likely, is to turn his back on family commitment, as his gaze shifts from Geneviève's shapely body to the open window, where he can see a new day dawning:

> Il sera bientôt temps que Geneviève le quitte; mais il attend encore; il écoute, penché sur elle, à travers son souffle léger, la vague rumeur de la ville qui déjà secoue sa torpeur. Au loin, dans les casernes, le clairon chante. Quoi! va-t-il renoncer à vivre? et pour l'estime de Geneviève, qu'il estime un peu moins depuis qu'elle l'aime un peu plus, songe-t-il encore à se livrer? (p. 250)[1]

The rhetorical questions placed in this concluding paragraph invite a negative answer. In the terms of the epitaph at the head of Book Five, Lafcadio has to accept that there are no easy solutions and that life must go on. Freedom cannot be definitively established in a single Romantic gesture, but has constantly to be rewon. 'Yes; strictly speaking, the question is not how to get cured, but how to live.' (p. 185)[2]

---

[1] It will soon be time for Geneviève to leave him; but still he waits; leaning over her, he listens above her gentle breathing to the vague rumour of the town as it begins to shake off its torpor. From the distant barracks a bugle's call rings out. What! is he going to renounce life? Does he still, for the sake of Geneviève's esteem (and already he esteems her a little less now that she loves him a little more), does he still think of giving himself up? (p. 237)

[2] p. 175.

Gide never advocated total freedom. Lafcadio's discovery should be a caution to us all, and his *acte gratuit*, if properly understood, need not cause concern. At most it should shock us into recognizing the enigma of the human psyche and the inadvisability of insufficient explanations of human behaviour. Aware that a completely motiveless crime is not possible, Gide is trying to show the need for action without thought of profit or gain. In terms of conventional morality based on outmoded psychological theories, such an action would *seem* unmotivated, simply because of the absence of a profit-motive to connect it with the agent or criminal.

> *Un être d'inconséquence*! c'est beaucoup dire . . . et sans doute cette apparente inconséquence cache-t-elle une séquence plus subtile et cachée; l'important c'est que ce qui le fasse agir, ce ne soit plus une simple raison d'intérêt ou, comme vous dites ordinairement: qu'ils n'obéissent plus à des motifs intéressés. (p. 175)[1]

In pointing to actions that are motivated 'par luxe, par besoin de dépense, par jeu' (p. 179),[2] Julius is summarizing the main features of Lafcadio's education by his 'uncles' and, in doing so, defines a psychological theory embodied in Lafcadio who is constantly open to contradictory impulses. Thus, Lafcadio's failure is only relative. He is the nearest we get in this comic novel to a sincere and authentic response to life. The ideal remains, and Lafcadio is given the opportunity to learn by his mistakes and proceed with the problem of living, which involves striving to give expression to all his natural feelings, ever mindful of the danger of insincere or calculated gestures.

---

[1] *A creature of inconsequence*! That's going rather far perhaps . . . and no doubt his apparent inconsequence hides, what is, in reality, a subtler and more recondite sequence – the important point is that what makes him act should not be a matter of interest, or, as the usual phrase is, that he should not be merely actuated by interested motives. (p. 164)

[2] 'out of extravagance – or the desire of a spendthrift, of a gambler.' (p. 169)

4

La Symphonie pastorale

La Symphonie pastorale is a *récit* in the manner of *L'Immoraliste* and *La Porte étroite* and, although it clearly reflects Gide's own religious and marital problems between 1916 and 1919, Gide saw it as his final debt to the past – a sort of throw-back to the intellectual and aesthetic concerns he experienced in the late 1890s. Like the two earlier *récits*, *La Symphonie pastorale* explores the tension between the conflicting impulses towards physical fulfilment and religious exaltation. The main protagonist, the pastor, is in fact an amalgam of Michel, Alissa and Jérôme. In his blindness and tendency towards self-delusion he echoes the confusion, seen in Jérôme, of worldly and otherworldly aims. Like Michel and Alissa, however, he refuses to acknowledge any authority other than his own individual conscience. His apparent callousness towards his wife and family and his defence of the liberating joy of physical experience and fulfilment against a narrow, conventional ethic are reminiscent of Michel. On the other hand, like Alissa, though with different motives, he justifies his personal choice with selective arguments drawn from the Gospels.

The plot of *La Symphonie pastorale* is extremely simple. A Protestant pastor takes into his home a blind, dumb girl and proceeds to neglect his wife and family as he devotes himself to the task of educating and civilizing his charge. This involves also training her imagination and stimulating her feelings as he interprets on her behalf the natural world which she cannot see. Because of this and because of his growing estrangement from family affairs, the pastor invests a great deal of emotional energy in his relationship with Gertrude, whom he comes to regard as his private concern. He is blind to the emotional strain his devotion to Gertrude places on his wife and forbids his son, Jacques, who is in love with her, to consider marrying her.

Thus, the pastor gradually comes to lead a double life as his high-minded intentions in respect of Gertrude give way to an ever-growing Romantic attachment to her. Her innocent love for him, which the reader sees as a reflection of the loving care he has stubbornly heaped on her, brings to the surface his own feelings of love. These he systematically justifies with casuistical interpretations of Gospel texts. Increasingly aware of the joy he derives from Gertrude's company, he cruelly neglects the emotional needs of his wife who, like Marceline in *L'Immoraliste* and Juliette in *La Porte étroite*, is the silent, suffering witness of her loved-one's private obsession.

Finally, Gertrude's *naïve* amoralism, based on values inculcated by the pastor, convinces him that sexual relations are the pure expression of their love. Afterwards, his instinctive sense of guilt is overridden by a grotesque process of rationalization according to which he manages to reconcile his adultery with his Christian duty. This moral blindness on the part of the pastor has been conditional upon Gertrude's sightlessness, which established her dependence on him. The recovery of her sight, as the pastor fears, destroys the artificial world of make-believe he has constructed, partly on her behalf, but also for his own ends. Immediately, Gertrude recognizes her guilt, regrets her earlier renunciation of Jacques and dies in despair.

The *récit* opens with no sense of an impending drama. It poses as an objective account of the educational and religious progress of a young girl, and the pastor's expression of gratitude to God, suggesting a willingness to accept a religious duty, seems in no way out of place. Similarly, the impression of drama, or even melodrama, created by his description of the first encounter with Gertrude, together with his sudden discovery of his Christian mission, contribute to an idea of fatality and the power of God's will. Finally, the pastor's sensitivity to Gertrude's predicament ('un être incertain, . . . cette pauvre abandonnée; . . . l'aveugle s'est laissée emmener comme une masse involontaire; . . . ce paquet de chair sans âme', pp. 15–18)[1] suggests his humanity and Christian charity in contrast to the harsh words of the neighbour, soon to be echoed by his own wife.

On the other hand, certain elements in the pastor's point of view can be detected. There is a tendency towards a Romantic interpretation of events, reinforced by key descriptions of the situation of the cottage ('un petit lac mystérieux; . . . dans l'enchantement rose et doré du soir; . . . une chaumière qu'on eût pu croire inhabitée, sans un mince filet de fumée qui s'en échappait, bleuissant dans l'ombre, puis blondissant dans l'or du ciel', pp. 12–13).[2] This Romantic sensitivity might easily be an aspect of his humanity and charitable concern. However, we also notice a rather self-conscious expression of religious aspirations and the habitual use of religious language:

> Hôtesse de ce corps opaque, une âme attend sans doute, emmurée, que vienne la toucher enfin quelque rayon de votre grâce, Seigneur! Permettrez-vous que mon amour, peut-être, écarte d'elle l'affreuse nuit. (p. 18)[3]

Underlying this is a sense of complacency and the implication that the pastor sees the lifeless creature as a personal test of his own faith. This is given some credence by the suggestion in the

[1] 'a nondescript-looking creature; . . . the poor, forlorn creature; . . . the blind girl allowed herself to be taken away like a lifeless block; . . . a soulless lump of flesh.' (pp. 11–12)

[2] 'a mysterious little lake; . . . in the golden enchantment of the rose-flecked evening sky; but for a tiny thread of smoke that rose from the chimney, looking blue in the shade and brightening as it reached the gold of the sky.' (pp. 9–10)

[3] But this darkened body is surely tenanted; an immured soul is waiting there for a ray of Thy grace, O Lord, to touch it to dispel this dreadful darkness. (p. 13)

conversation with the neighbour that he is looking for the approval of others and is partly motivated by a desire to prove that they are wrong in their scepticism.

Thus, in this opening section there is a superficial impression created by the pastor himself of his Christian charity, modified by vague suggestions of other, hidden, motives. These are confirmed in the pastor's description of the welcome he received from his family. We note his harsh judgement of Amélie's limited capacity for charity (although the confusion caused by Gertrude's arrival seems entirely justifiable) and, despite agreeing with her complaints concerning his thoughtlessness and impracticability, he proceeds to argue his way skilfully out of a bad position. Above all, his Christian smugness and pomposity is once again underlined as he quotes from the parable of the lost sheep and regrets that he cannot exploit Gertrude's arrival to give his children a lesson in Christian charity. This critical view of the pastor's attitudes is completed by his noticeably uncharitable judgement of his daughter, Charlotte, and by his own admission of his growing despair as he contrasts his Quixotic intentions with Gertrude's complete unresponsiveness.

The psychological theories of Dr Martins play a crucial role in reviving the pastor's enthusiasm in so far as they provide a real model for him to emulate. In the pastor's educational programme, there is still a confusion of motives: and, as the pastor criticizes his wife's lack of faith in the light of his own literal interpretation of the parable of the lost sheep, his joy at Gertrude's first smile has, beneath a superficial religiosity, all the accents of the awakening of romantic love:

> Tout à coup ses traits s'animèrent; ce fut comme un éclairement subit, pareil à cette lueur pourpurine dans les hautes Alpes qui, précédant l'aurore, fait vibrer le sommet neigeux qu'elle désigne et sort de la nuit; on eût dit une coloration mystique; et je songeai également à la

piscine de Bethesda au moment que l'ange descend et vient
réveiller l'eau dormante. J'eus une sorte de ravissement
devant l'expression angélique que Gertrude put prendre
soudain. . . . Alors un tel élan de reconnaissance me sou-
leva, qu'il me sembla que j'offrai à Dieu le baiser que je
déposai sur ce beau front. (pp. 42–3)[1]

The depth of feeling here is clearly directed at Gertrude, with
whom the pastor becomes totally obsessed, as the loss of
control in his account would suggest.

It is soon clear that Gertrude is quite dependent on the pastor
for an interpretation of the natural world, and his possible
inadequacy in this task is seen in the difficulty over the question
of colours, as well as in her plea for honesty when she wants
him to confirm that the world she *imagines* under the stimu-
lation of the *Pastoral Symphony* is a faithful reflection of the
real world. The strong suggestion in this scene that Gertrude
is the victim of her dependence on the pastor is reinforced by
a restatement of Amélie's grievances which, in his moral
superiority, the pastor does not bother to answer, contenting
himself privately with a series of feeble rationalizations.

In contrast to his devotion to Gertrude, then, we note his
refusal to face up to his responsibilities to Amélie. Again, he is
extremely *literal* as well as blind in his analysis of her behaviour, wishing to restrict his guilt to the trivial question of
the forgotten reel of thread, so that he can ascribe her more
general concern at his obsession with Gertrude to the uncontrolled workings of her imagination. In this process of self-
deception he takes visible refuge in another religious text,

[1] Her features flashed into life – a sudden illumination, like the crimson
glow that precedes dawn in the high Alps, thrilling the snowy peak on
which it lights and calling it up out of darkness – such a flood, it seemed,
of mystic colour; and I thought too of the pool of Bethesda at the moment
the angel descends to stir the slumbering water. A kind of ecstasy rapt me
at the sight of the angelic expression that came over Gertrude's face so
suddenly . . . And in a very transport of gratitude I kissed her forehead and
felt that I was offering thanks to God. (p. 24)

seeing his wife's predicament as no more than a suitable
subject for a sermon and as an unwarranted intrusion into his
account of Gertrude's development:

> Ah! que la vie serait belle et notre misère supportable, si
> nous nous contentions des maux réels sans prêter l'oreille
> aux fantômes et aux monstres de notre esprit . . . Mais je
> me laisse aller à noter ici ce qui ferait plutôt le sujet d'un
> sermon (Matt. [*sic*] XII, 29 'N'ayez point l'esprit inquiet').
> C'est l'histoire du développement intellectuel et moral de
> Gertrude que j'ai entrepris de tracer ici. J'y reviens.
> (pp. 64–5)[1]

The same process of self-deception is seen in his grotesque
appeal to conscience in order to persuade Jacques to renounce
Gertrude – a fact highlighted by Jacques' own impeccable
attitude towards Gertrude and his father and by the pastor's
admission that, were Gertrude not blind, she could not have
failed to be impressed by Jacques' appearance. And in the
following encounter with Amélie the pastor's brutal mis-
interpretation of her motives when she tries to warn him
obliquely of the dangers of his obsession with Gertrude, leads
to a momentary regret at his harsh words and to the uncharitable and wrong assumption that her displeasure and anxiety
are directed at Gertrude rather than at himself. His total
blindness to the pathos of Amélie's situation is graphically
illustrated by his return to Gertrude and the ironical gap
between his pious intentions and his abandonment of Amélie
for Gertrude:

> *Je m'étais imposé ce devoir* de consacrer quotidiennement

---

[1] Ah! how beautiful life would be and how bearable our wretchedness if
we were content with real evils, without opening the doors to the phantoms
and monsters of our imagination. . . . But I am straying here into obser-
vations that would do better as the subject of a sermon – (Luke, xii. 29:
'Neither be ye of doubtful mind'). It is the history of Gertrude's intellectual
and moral development that I purposed tracing here and I must now return
to it. (p. 34)

un peu de temps à Gertrude; c'était, suivant les occupations de chaque jour, *quelques heures* ou quelques instants. *Le lendemain du jour* où j'avais eu cette conversation avec *Amélie*, je me trouvais assez libre, et, le beau temps y invitant, j'entraînais *Gertrude* à travers la forêt '. . . (p. 89)[1]

It is in this scene that the pastor's behaviour becomes the ironical parallel of that of the deluded hero of Dickens's *The Cricket on the Hearth*, who had been mentioned, presumably as a warning, by Dr Martins earlier in the *récit*. The pastor allows Gertrude's imaginings to take the place of reality. Not only this, he also exploits her Romantic identity with the natural world in order that he may escape from everyday reality, in Baudelairean fashion, into an exotic, unreal haven of rest. We note in this connexion the striking contrast between his muted and relatively factual description of the spot and Gertrude's metaphorical enthusiasm, revealing her attachment to what is, literally, a pathetic fallacy:

Une prairie à l'herbe à la fois rase et drue dévalait à nos pieds; plus loin pâturaient quelques vaches; chacune d'elles, dans ce troupeau de montagne, porte une cloche au cou . . . (p. 90)

A nos pieds, comme un livre ouvert, incliné sur le pupitre de la montagne, la grande prairie verte et diaprée que bleuit l'ombre, que dore le soleil et dont les mots distincts sont des fleurs – des gentianes, des pulsatilles, des renoncules, et les beaux lys de Salomon – que les vaches viennent épeler avec leurs cloches, et où les anges

---

[1] (My italics, CDB) *I had imposed on myself the duty* of devoting *a little time* daily to Gertrude – *a few hours* or a few minutes, according to the occupations in hand. *The day after* this conversation with *Amélie*, I had some free time, and as the weather was inviting, I took *Gertrude* with me through the forest . . . (p. 45)

viennent lire, puisque vous dites que les yeux des hommes
sont clos ... (p. 93)[1]

In encouraging Gertrude to believe that she possesses the
superior perception of the angels, the pastor encourages the
sin of pride and, at the same time, uses Gertrude's innocence
to pander to his own emotional needs. For, in addition, he
makes no attempt to correct Gertrude's mistaken impression
that, being blind, she cannot expect marriage, and which leads
her to assume that she must look for happiness wherever she
can find it.

At the beginning of the Second Notebook, the pastor brings
his retrospective account up to the present and summarizes
his present state of awareness. The ironical gap between the
pastor's imperfect self-knowledge and the reader's greater
understanding of the situation is greater than ever. Significantly, he is still blind to his wife's point of view. That is to say,
he has not become aware of the moral implications of his
actions: he does not regret his love, but regrets only that he
did not *recognize* it earlier. Thus, he still remains unaware of
the symbolic implications of taking communion with Gertrude
on Easter Day while Jacques and Amélie look on and he, full
of pious superiority, prays for Amélie to end her spiritual
isolation. He can validate his own selective reading of the
Gospels only by insisting on Jacques' dogmatism and lack of
humanity.

On his side, the pastor claims the sanction of freedom,
plenitude and perfect happiness and contrasts his attachment

---

[1] A meadow of thick, closely cropped grass sloped downwards at our
feet; further off, a few cows were grazing; each of them among these
mountain herds wears a bell at its neck ... (p. 46)

At our feet, like an open book on the sloping desk of the mountain, lies
the broad green meadow, shot with shifting colours – blue in the shade,
golden in the sun, and speaking in clear words of flowers – gentians,
pulsatillas, ranunculus and Solomon's beautiful lilies; the cows come and
spell them out with their bells; and the angels come and read them – for
you say that the eyes of men are closed ... (p. 47)

to these with what he assumes to be Jacques' perverse insistence on submission and sinfulness. Also striking is the pastor's increased dependence on what are clearly very self-interested interpretations of Gospel texts that are so ambiguous that they could quite easily be used against him. Ironically, he has recourse to La Rochefoucauld but the quotation he aims at Jacques is perfectly illustrative of his own position. Whenever literal interpretations are unhelpful, the pastor turns to any sense provided it is dictated by love: in fact, these interpretations are dictated not by divine love, but by love of Gertrude.

The pernicious effects of the pastor's blindness and self-indulgence are seen in three successive accounts of Jacques (pp. 110–13), Amélie and the children (pp. 113–17), and the household of Mlle de M . . . (pp. 117–20).[1] In the first, as we have already indicated, we become aware of the pastor's blatant casuistry as he attempts to equate his adulterous love with the Gospel message. This is immediately followed by his renewed attack on the inadequacy of his wife and family to provide him with 'un exigeant besoin de repos, d'affection, de chaleur' (p. 115),[2] and leads on to his idealization of a substitute family life experienced at the house of Mlle de M. . . .

In the subsequent encounter with Gertrude, the pastor cannot stand up to the logic of Gertrude's arguments as she forces him to envisage the sexual consummation of their relationship in the name of values he has encouraged her to accept. At a key moment in this scene Gertrude uses arguments provided by the pastor to define *their* love (an answer to the pastor's 'ton amour', p. 128)[3] as in keeping with God's law of love. Although it is clear that the pastor has already argued this way with Jacques, his reluctance to face up to the physical consequences of his wayward thinking is seen in his feeble

---

[1] pp. 54–6, 56–8, 58–9.
[2] 'a longing for rest, affection, warmth' (p. 57)
[3] p. 63.

attempts to counter her proposal and in his willingness to pose as the victim of her ardour. In this scene the reader becomes clearly aware of the ironic contrast between the pastor and Gertrude in the matter of morality. The pastor's moralistic self-justifications derive from his recognition that the absolute moral teaching of his Church is irreconcilable with his instinctive love for Gertrude. For this reason the new morality he seeks to advocate relates only to his private emotional requirements. With Gertrude, however, things are quite different. Her love for the pastor, apparently instinctive, has in fact been actively encouraged and nurtured by the pastor. In her mind there is a conflict between this and a purer moral sense that she has discovered quite independently of the pastor – one that relates not only to her own individual happiness but also to that of Amélie and the pastor's children.

What emerges at this point is the pathos of Gertrude's situation as she struggles to choose between this instinctive sense of responsibility towards Amélie and, prompted by her blindness, a desire to find what earthly happiness she can. Her blindness, therefore, is the precondition of their love, and we are reminded forcefully of the pastor's dishonesty in not telling her of Dr Martin's desire to operate (p. 109).[1] This is underlined by the juxtaposition of his refusal to tell her that she is operable and the adulterous visit to her bedroom, which depends on her belief that she will never regain her sight. The pastor's dishonesty in this respect is given further emphasis by the marked understatement and extreme simplicity of the pastor's account of the visit to Gertrude's bedroom. We note, too, the attempt of the pastor to convince himself that his action has divine sanction and his extreme apprehension at Gertrude's return from hospital. When she returns, her sense of guilt gives rise to her attempt at suicide and to her conversion, with Jacques, to Catholicism. Right to the last, however, the pastor's eyes are not fully open to his guilt and it is not

[1] p. 54.

clear whether, even at her death, he fully understands his moral responsibility in all that has occurred, for the overriding impression given is simply one of despair at the loss of her love.

Thus far in our analysis we have laid great emphasis on the pastor's blindness and on the tragic consequences of his selfishness and complacency. But *La Symphonie pastorale* is more than the unmasking of a religious hypocrite, however unwitting. It is also an open discussion about the nature of innocence and, in addition, an unusual kind of love story set, like all great romantic stories, in extremely unfavourable circumstances. Of course, the moral perspective through which the reader views the pastor's blindness is dominant in the book, and the presentation of events in terms of a doomed romantic love may simply be another dimension of the pastor's attempt to seek justification for his conduct. On the other hand, our critical judgement of the pastor should, perhaps, be modified by the ways by which Gide seeks to make us understand and even sympathize with the pastor.

In the tragedies of Racine, we may remember, a tragic hero provokes hostility and, sometimes, moral outrage, but also pity. *Phèdre*, for example, may well be an illustration of the pernicious effects of an uncontrolled passion. Its heroine may resort to crime and revolt against the moral order in order to validate her love, but the very strength of this love and, more importantly, the way in which she expresses her commitment to what is objectively nothing more than an impossible dream produces an irresistible sense of pathos. At certain moments the audience is asked to identify, if only a little, with her irrational aims.

La Symphonie pastorale has something of the same effect. In the first place, to experience events through the mind of the principal protagonist leads to a certain dependence on his point of view. His picture of the relative joylessness of family life is almost certainly not entirely Amélie's fault, contrary to what the pastor wishes to suggest; but, nevertheless, the pastor

sometimes seems justified in his desire to break out of a stulti-
fying family routine. In other words, the impulses the pastor
feels are entirely valid in themselves, even if they lead on this
occasion to disastrous social consequences. In addition, the
pastor's unrestrained excitement at Gertrude's progress is
expressed in a persuasive poetic prose the beauty of which
reveals, besides his growing obsession with Gertrude, a capacity for enthusiasm and a delicacy of feeling that Gide does
not trivialize:

> Chaque fois que je la retrouvais, c'était avec une nouvelle
> surprise et je me sentais séparé d'elle par une moindre
> épaisseur de nuit. C'est tout de même ainsi, me disais-je,
> que la tiédeur de l'air et l'insistance du printemps triomph-
> ent peu à peu de l'hiver. Que de fois n'ai-je pas admiré
> la manière dont fond la neige: on dirait que le manteau
> s'use par en dessous, et son aspect reste le même. A
> chaque hiver, Amélie y est prise et me déclare: la neige
> n'a toujours pas changé; on la croit épaisse encore quand
> déjà la voici qui cède et tout à coup, de place en place,
> laisse reparaître la vie. (p. 44)[1]

The pleasure the pastor takes in her pleasure and his loving
descriptions of her face and her every gesture are striking as
his attitude changes imperceptibly from pity and pastoral concern to perfect companionship and love. He proves to be a
whimsical and sensitive interpreter of the Alpine scene:

> A quoi les comparerai-je aujourd'hui? A la soif d'un

---

[1] Every time I came back to her after an absence, it was to find with fresh
surprise that the wall of darkness that separated us had grown less thick.
After all, I said to myself, it is so that the warmth of the air and the
insistence of spring gradually triumph over winter. How often have I
wondered at the melting of the snow; its white cloak seems to wear thin
from underneath, while to all appearance it remains unchanged. Every
winter Amélie falls into the trap: 'The snow is as thick as ever,' she de-
clares. And indeed it seems so, when all at once there comes a break and
suddenly, in patches here and there, life once more shows through. (p. 25)

plein jour d'été. Avant ce soir elles auront achevé de se dissoudre dans l'air. (p. 90)[1]

And in Gertrude's description of lilies of the field we see that the pastor has managed to communicate this poetic sense:

On dirait des cloches de flamme, de grandes cloches d'azur emplies du parfum de l'amour et que balance le vent du soir. (pp. 91–2)[2]

In her company the pastor becomes rejuvenated and feels younger than his son, and in the process become transformed into the romantic lover:

Nous marchions vite; l'air vif colorait ses joues et ramenait sans cesse sur son visage ses cheveux blonds. Comme nous longions une tourbière, je cueillis quelques joncs en fleurs, dont je glissai les tiges sous son béret, puis que je tressai avec ses cheveux pour les maintenir. (pp. 122–3)[3]

Finally, the pastor's longing for divine justification as he struggles to blot from his mind his sense of guilt at his adultery is deeply moving and harrowing:

L'air est tiède et par ma fenêtre ouverte la lune entre et j'écoute le silence immense des cieux. O confus adoration de la création toute entière où fond mon cœur dans une extase sans paroles. Je ne peux plus prier qu'éperdument. . . . Pour coupable que mon amour paraisse aux yeux des hommes, oh! dites-moi qu'aux vôtres il est saint. (p. 131)[4]

---

[1] 'What shall I compare them to this afternoon? To a thirsty midsummer's day. Before evening they will have melted into the air.' (p. 46)

[2] They are like bells of flame – great bells of azure, filled with the perfume of love and swinging in the evening breeze. (p. 47)

[3] We walked quickly; the sharp air coloured her cheeks and kept blowing her fair hair over her face. As we passed alongside a peat-moss, I picked one or two rushes that were in flower and slipped the stalks under her béret; then I twined them into her hair so as to keep them in place. (p. 60)

[4] The air is warm and the moon shines in at my open window as I sit listening to the vast silence of the skies. Oh, from all creation rises a blended adoration which bears my heart along, lost in an ecstasy that knows no words. I cannot – I cannot pray with calm. . . . However guilty my love may appear in the eyes of men, oh, tell me that in Thine, it is sacred. (p. 64)

Thus, while the pastor's moral blindness has a noticeably harmful effect on the lives of Amélie, Jacques and Gertrude, there is in the Second Notebook a certain sense of grandeur and a Romantic force, coupled with an awful sense of waste, not only in respect of Amélie, Gertrude and Jacques, but also in respect of the pastor himself. For Gide's great achievement in all three of his *récits* was to balance critical distance with sympathy, ironical detachment with emotional attachment and to combine classical control with Romantic enthusiasm. This is particularly true of *La Symphonie pastorale* and it is no mean achievement.

5

Les Faux-Monnayeurs

(i) *Themes*

The counterfeiters in the title of Gide's novel are a small gang of schoolboys organized by a sinister, cynical figure, Strouvilhou, whose activities have marked repercussions on the major characters of the novel. But the title also signifies, in a figurative sense, the various forms of hypocrisy and bad faith displayed by nearly all the characters in their relationships with each other. Each lives in a mental world of his own construction, interpreting reality and external events either in the light of his own self-interest or in relation to attitudes imposed on him by others. These can include conventional religious and social attitudes deemed desirable, exaggerated reactions of revolt against social norms and, even, a proto-Sartrian *mauvaise foi*, in which a character conforms to the view another has of him.

Thus, as in *Les Caves du Vatican*, characters act out roles for the benefit of others. They may act in unwitting complicity, like Profitendieu and Molinier in Part One, chapter two, or they may engage, like Edouard and Passavant, in a furious duel of wits in the desire to impress a third person, Olivier Molinier (Part Three, chapter eight). In fact, Passavant is involved in further encounters of this kind with Strouvilhou and then with the even more extreme Cob-Lafleur. Even close relationships are affected by this spirit of rivalry, which leads to the adoption of poses for effect. An example of this is the relationship between Olivier and Bernard in Part Two. Bernard's sincere and undisguised delight in the company of

Edouard (chapter one) leads Olivier, out of jealousy, to exaggerate the credit of Passavant. His true motives are revealed in the postscript to the letter which is imperfectly scratched out.

Between Edouard and Laura the communication gap is even greater, emphasized by the fact that they had been in love and nearly married. They had not done so because Edouard, feeling himself an unsuitable match, had encouraged Laura to marry Félix Douviers. An indirect consequence of Edouard's action was Laura's affair with Vincent Molinier and, when abandoned by him, Laura seeks Edouard's protection. He indeed rallies to her aid but is incredibly awkward and distant in her company, and the frustrations that this creates in the mind of Laura are subtly analysed in the third chapter of Part Two. Edouard's shortcomings in this respect are highlighted by Bernard's exaggerated imitation of them in chapter fourteen of Part One, when sincere feelings of sympathy break through in the midst of the heroic gesture of support Bernard is making. Gide draws the same distinction between spontaneous and false behaviour during Edouard's encounter with Profitendieu, when the old man briefly abandons calculations of professional and personal self-interest to express real distress at Bernard's rejection of his family.

Society is severely judged through the interaction of the members of three family groups, the Profitendieus, the Moliniers and the Vedel-Azaïs. The older generation, including magistrates, pastors, teachers and their wives, forms one important group of characters for whom conventional attitudes must be preserved at all costs. A middle group, which includes Bernard Profitendieu, Vincent and Olivier Molinier and the Vedel children, is seen at different stages of coming to grips with the adult world. Beneath these there is a group of young teenagers, all of them pupils at the Azaïs school, who are exposed to the influence of cultural and social anarchists, like Strouvilhou and Dhurmer, just as the middle group is tempted by the cynical outsiders, Passavant, Lady Griffith, Miss Aberdeen and, to a certain degree, Edouard.

For Edouard is involved at different moments in all three of these worlds, both as an actor and as the detached observer of a reality he is attempting to circumscribe in his projected novel. His literary aims reflect those of Gide himself and he is also the mouthpiece of Gide's views on social morality on two levels: he observes the hypocrisy and insincerity of others – Profitendieu, Molinier, Vedel and Passavant – and occasionally gives evidence of his own; and he comments on this in his search for more original and sincere behaviour in the young – Bernard, Olivier and, finally, Caloub.

Edouard, a bachelor and homosexual, is the privileged witness of the inadequacy of marriage as a social institution. In a series of conversations with Profitendieu, Paula and Oscar Molinier and old La Pérouse, he observes the harrowing effects of human conflict and misunderstanding. In the aberrant behaviour of Georges and Vincent Molinier, Alexander and Sarah Vedel and the schoolboys organized by Strouvilhou and Ghérandisol, there is further evidence of the inability of family life to provide a moral and religious background strong enough to resist the influence of Passavant, Lady Griffith and their like. Indeed, the desire of Profitendieu and Molinier to protect Georges Molinier and his friends from normal police procedures establishes an ironical coincidence of interests with Strouvilhou and a justification of Passavant's cynicism.

It is in the description of the Vedel household that the moral bankruptcy of the bourgeois family is most precisely identified. The relationship between the hypocritical Prosper and his wife, Mélanie, parallels the marriages of Profitendieu and Molinier. His children all react against this thoroughgoing Puritanism, but their systematic rejection of parental values is, ironically, no more satisfactory. Alexandre's profligacy, Laura's extra-marital adventure with Vincent, Sarah's aggressive sexuality, Armand's cynicism and Rachel's mindless self-sacrifice are all

perverted reactions to a twisted family milieu that also shelters
Strouvilhou, himself the perverter of the young schoolboys in
their moral charge. In addition, there is, in the closely connected
family of La Pérouse, an exaggeration of the same tendencies,
dramatically focused on old La Pérouse and his grandson,
Boris.

Gide's answer to the illegitimacy, infidelity and inhumanity
that characterize conventional family life is to present as more
normal and more life-enhancing a number of homosexual
relationships, real or potential. Passavant's clearsighted
seduction of Olivier with the help of Vincent does not destroy
the impression of 'normal' human love felt between Bernard
and Olivier, and Edouard and Olivier. Much of the action of
the novel concerns the complex love-lives of four characters,
Laura, Vincent Molinier, Bernard and Edouard. Edouard's
original rejection of Laura for Olivier leads to her loveless
marriage with Douviers and to the ultimate failure of her
relationship with Vincent (who turns to Lady Griffith) as well
as to an inability to respond to Bernard (who turns to Sarah).
While all of these heterosexual relationships lead to dissatisfaction or disaster, Edouard's affair with Olivier has a privileged status, surviving seduction by Passavant and the attempted suicide of Olivier to receive the final sanction of
Olivier's mother.

On the other hand, Edouard does not escape identification
with the counterfeiters of the novel. He, too, is dominated by
his own partial attitude towards life based on his detachment
and love of abstractions. As Bernard notices, Edouard has a
tendency to adjust facts and events to fit his own ideas, whereas
Bernard is what Edouard would call a realist who adjusts his
ideas to fit with the facts. Seen in this way, it is Bernard and not
Edouard who represents, like Lafcadio in *Les Caves du Vatican*,
Gide's examination of the possibility of authentic, sincere
behaviour. He is more real than the other characters and is
made to pass through a number of crucial experiences of life

before he takes the free decision to return to his family home in order to console his father.

What Bernard rejects is a way of life outside the family that is in fact no more sincere than what it is seeking to react against. The reactions of Sarah, Armand and Vincent, for example, are mechanical responses to certain social conditions and have no particular moral significance. The same point is made about the systematic immoralism of Lady Griffith, Passavant and Strouvilhou, who encourage this sort of revolt against society for their own purposes. Ironically, Vedel's hypocrisy and Bernard's sincerity produce the same effect, insincerity in others.

(ii) *Action and Interaction*

Les Faux-Monnayeurs is divided into three parts, with eighteen chapters in each of Parts One and Three and a central section of seven chapters. Part One is set in Paris and most of the action is concentrated symbolically on the *sixième arrondissement*, the home of the wealthy upper middle class. In the first seven chapters all possible illusions we might have about the values of family life are relentlessly stripped away as the reader is confronted with the disillusionment of Bernard on discovering his bastardy (chapter one), the hypocritical concern of Profitendieu and Molinier about a case of adolescent immorality (chapter two), and the brutal rejection by Vincent Molinier of his pregnant mistress (chapters three and four). Further details about existing relationships are revealed in Passavant's discussion with Lady Griffith (chapter five). The latter has lured Vincent from Laura, who is presented as her pathetic victim. As Bernard, after sleeping with Olivier, envisages a new life (chapter six), Vincent awakens in Lady Griffith's bed to hear her story of the shipwreck of the *Bourgogne* (chapter seven), which emphasizes her cynical philosophy of life and at the same symbolizes the jungle morality of society, to which we have already been introduced.

There is a complete change of perspective with the appearance in chapter eight of Edouard, novelist and half-brother of Olivier's mother. Defined in opposition to the successful Passavant, he is returning to protect Laura, whom he had himself nearly married. He is also Passavant's rival for the love of Olivier Molinier (chapter nine) and this in turn arouses the jealousy of Olivier's friend, Bernard (chapter ten). When Bernard secretly reads Edouard's diary (chapters eleven, twelve, thirteen) he discovers significant facts and details about which he cannot know the significance but which reinforce the thematic unity of the earlier part of the novel and point to later developments in Part Three. Noteworthy is his discovery of Edouard's connexion with the third family group, the Vedel-Azaïs, who provide a Protestant variation on the shortcomings of the Profitendieus and the Moliniers. A circular movement is completed with the allusions to the subject of Edouard's projected novel, *Les Faux-Monnayeurs*, which is to study the nightmarish prison of family life, from which only the bastard can escape.

Having broken away from his family, Bernard in fact tries to commit himself to family problems by offering his protection to Laura (chapter fourteen), thus providing with his youthful ardour an ironical counterpoint to Edouard's embarrassment. While he persuades Edouard to employ him as his secretary, Passavant, in a parallel movement (chapters fifteen and seventeen), gets Vincent's help to persuade the Moliniers to allow Olivier to accompany him as his secretary.

The tight network of interpersonal relationships established in Part One is emphasized by Bernard's delight at coincidence (Part Two, chapter one) and by Edouard's interest in the fictional possibilities of Bernard. Clearly the three closely related families symbolize society as a whole. The hypocrisy and inadequacy of the adult members – judges, pastors, doctors and teachers – match the cynicism of the aristocrats, Lady Griffith and Passavant. This is given striking confirmation in the predicament of Laura, whose fate is symbolized by the little girl saved by Lady Griffith before the latter's natural charity had become perverted by the shipwreck experience.

We see the young in the process of being transformed into social animals. This is illustrated in the corruption of the sons of gentlefolk by Dhurmer, and dramatically counterpointed by his friend Passavant's abduction of Olivier. Vincent, the young doctor, is poised between natural feelings of guilt and imitation of the inhumanity of Lady Griffith, and his seduction by her is echoed in the behaviour of Sarah Vedel towards Olivier (chapter twelve). Furthermore, Vincent's change of attitude is symbolized by his rejection of medicine (= care and concern for others) in favour of biology, with its emphasis on Darwinian theories of natural selection.

Some of the time Bernard and Edouard seem to inhabit neutral ground, from which the workings of society are viewed. But hints concerning the limitations of Edouard's viewpoint should not be missed: his detached amusement at Georges Molinier's theft of a book; his embarrassment in the company of Laura and Bernard; his casual reaction to old La Pérouse's suicide plan; and the fact that his grasp of the total situation comes after that of Bernard. Bernard, too, is in danger of being drawn, through contact with Edouard and Laura, back into the family circle from which he had intended to escape.

There is a natural shift from Paris in Part One to Saas-Fée in Part Two by way of the conversation between Edouard and old La Pérouse in chapter eighteen. The action of Part Two is framed by an exchange of letters between Olivier and Bernard. Bernard's idyllic description of his life with Laura and Edouard (chapter one) provokes Olivier's jealousy and drives him further into the orbit of Passavant. In Olivier's reply (chapter six) his enthusiasm for Passavant echoes Bernard's admiration for Edouard, but a clear contrast is established between Bernard's sincerity and Olivier's hurt pride. In a similar way a moral judgement is implicit in the contrast between

Edouard's introduction of Bernard to the pleasures of moun-
taineering and Passavant's introduction of Olivier to the world
of fine clothes, theatres and prostitutes.

The treatment of Boris by Bronja, described by Edouard in
chapter two, throws further light on the treatment Laura has
received from her different admirers. In love with Edouard,
she finds herself adored by Bernard, whose offer of love she
refuses out of duty to her forgiving husband (chapter four).
Douviers' behaviour here brings Bernard back to a momentary
reassessment of his own illegitimacy, but the revolt against
family hypocrisy once again comes to the fore. And suddenly,
in the course of this conversation, an ironical gap is opened
out between Bernard's *absolute* demands and Laura's relativism,
according to which she can love Edouard, Douviers and
Bernard in different ways.

Bernard's love for Laura is partly determined by his oft-
repeated dissatisfaction with Edouard's procrastination and
with frustration at not being fully stretched by his job as
secretary. This conviction of Edouard's inadequacy as a
novelist takes up the lengthy discussions between Laura,
Edouard, Bernard and the psychologist, Mme Sophroniska
(chapter three) and links up with the extracts from Edouard's
diary (chapter five) and with the intervention by Gide himself
(chapter seven). Sophroniska's scepticism about the novelist's
art (pp. 177–8) is balanced by Edouard's suspicion of the
methods of psychoanalysis (pp. 190–1, 205–6).[1] Edouard's
belief that Sophroniska's methods might be counter-productive
is ironically linked in the reader's mind with the fact that
Edouard's generous treatment of Bernard and Laura has not
been wholly appreciated and with the suggestion of cruelty
(chapter seven) in Edouard's plan to send Boris to the Vedel-
Azaïs school.

In the discussion about Edouard's projected novel, the
would-be author gropes towards the elaboration of fictional

[1] pp. 161–2, 173–4, 187–8.

notions that clearly apply to Gide's novel. We note his desire for originality, his criticism of Balzacian and realist claims to present a faithful image of reality, and his admiration for the powerfully human significance of the stylized classical dramas of Corneille, Molière and Racine. The central problem in Edouard's novel will be the struggle of his novelist-hero to come to grips with reality. The scepticism shown by Laura and Bernard towards Edouard's new theories which seem based on a desire to get back at Passavant is not shared by the author who, in chapter seven, subjects all of his characters to a number of criticisms. These simply clarify impressions that have arisen naturally in the course of Parts One and Two and, at the same time, suggest a relationship between author and characters implicit in Edouard's artistic intentions.

The action of Part Three returns to Paris. Seen by Gide at the end of Part Two as part of an experiment set up by Edouard, events are framed by entries in his diary. There is a return in the first chapter to Judge Molinier, the husband of Edouard's half-sister, Pauline. Molinier speaks of his own infidelity to his wife and blindly congratulates his children on their choice of friends, the Prince of Monaco, Passavant and Adamanti, and runs down Bernard, accusing him of complicity in the scandal at the Azaïs school described in the opening pages of the novel. Thus, in this chapter there is a restatement of the principal themes and relationships of Part One, reiterated in the conversations in the Vedel household (chapter two), in which the inhumanity of family life is epitomized in the role of Rachel. Her devotion to the family and the sacrifices she has made on behalf of Laura and their brother, Alexandre, are appreciated only by another brother, Armand, whose cynicism, like the naïve surprise of Bernard in Part One, is the touchstone for Gide's criticism of family values. The picture of the Vedel family is completed by the arrival of Sarah (chapter eight) who revolts against conventional moral scruples and spends the night with Bernard. Finally, Edouard's interview with old

La Pérouse recalls the encounter in Part One. There is grim pathos here as the old man describes his wife's hostility and his own failure to commit suicide, thus reinforcing the picture of the Vedels.

Further developments are seen in the three-way relationship between Bernard, Edouard and Olivier and we note a reversal of the events of Part One. Bernard and Olivier are reconciled (pp. 262–7)[1] after a fractious interview (pp. 254–8).[2] After the literary banquet at which both Passavant and Edouard are present (chapter eight), Olivier returns to Edouard with whom he sleeps and then promptly attempts to commit suicide. Curiously, Pauline Molinier gives her approval to the relationship between her son and her half-brother (pp. 305–10).[3] This meeting relates back to an earlier meeting (chapter six) when Pauline discussed her relationship with Judge Molinier and expressed concern for Olivier and Georges – a contrast to her husband's views discussed with Edouard in chapter one.

Edouard's rivalry with Passavant over Olivier is closely connected with the influence of Passavant's associates, Dhurmer and Strouvilhou, over the boys at the Azaïs school. This establishment represents society in miniature in that it houses Georges Molinier, Gontran de Passavant, Boris, Bernard Profitendieu and old La Pérouse, as well as Philippe Adamanti, the son of a Corsican senator.

Strouvilhou, aided by his cousin, Ghérandisol, persuades the others to help him circulate counterfeit coins. As a protection against conviction he has a number of documents confirming the sexual peccadilloes of Profitendieu, Molinier and Boris's family. Strouvilhou's conversation with Passavant (chapter eleven) involves a restatement of Lady Griffith's attitude to life. Based on a systematic rejection of the Christian values of charity and humanitarian concern, his Nietzschean aspirations for human progress at the expense of the weak are

[1] pp. 239–43.   [2] pp. 231–5.   [3] pp. 279–82.

combined with a total disregard for conventional literature, the artificiality of which he intends to expose in the new literary journal he hopes to edit. With this aim Strouvilhou and Edouard meet on some sort of common ground. This is emphasized by Edouard's diary entries (chapter twelve) concerning his dislike of consistent characters in novels. Edouard's approach is, however, in complete contrast to Strouvilhou, extremely hesitant and academic.

Edouard is involved in all the major crises in Part Three. In his company Olivier challenges Dhurmer to a duel and then tries to commit suicide. He then has to dissuade Douviers from challenging Vincent to a duel over the pregnancy of his wife, Laura. Finally he has an uncomfortable interview (pp. 325–30)[1] with Profitendieu who tells him of Georges Molinier's new involvement with a gang of counterfeiters. Sent to warn Georges in the hope of avoiding a scandal, Edouard unwittingly sets off a chain of events organized by Strouvilhou and his associates.

The predatory Lady Griffith and Strouvilhou are succeeded by Ghérandisol, whose victim is Boris, now distraught at the death of Bronja.

The setting for this final crisis is the Azaïs school, where Boris and La Pérouse are already persecuted and victimized by the inmates. Boris is inveigled into performing an initiation rite in which he is to feign a suicide attempt in order to frighten old La Pérouse, using the same pistol the old man had once wished to use. The pistol is loaded and Boris kills himself, while La Pérouse is paralysed by a stroke.

Ironically, Edouard is disturbed by the apparent lack of motivation of the suicide and by the effect it has on the future of the Azaïs-Vedel, on the Moliniers and even on Armand Vedel. Edouard's distaste for the event and his detached account of the effects of Boris's suicide is shocking in the light

[1] pp. 296–301.

of his own role in the affair. We remember his lack of concern at La Pérouse's suicide plan with the loaded pistol, his responsibility in bringing both Boris and La Pérouse to the Azaïs school and his failure to influence Georges Molinier to end his association with Strouvilhou and Ghérandisol. If we add to this Bernard's departure from the school (depriving Boris of his support) and the inability of Boris to find the comfort of friendship with Gontran de Passavant and Philippe Adamanti, we have, in fact, a concerted conspiracy of social and anti-social forces against the pathetic figure of Boris. It is clear that the evil influence of Strouvilhou and Ghérandisol is predicated on the inadequacy and hypocrisy of society, and this is underlined by Profitendieu's deliberate delay of police action in order that the Moliniers can save face – a delay that made Ghérandisol's victimization of Boris more possible.

In an apparently pessimistic final paragraph there is a return to the state of affairs at the beginning of the book. The bourgeois family once again closes ranks. Bernard is reconciled with his father; Pauline returns to Molinier and, with her sons Georges and Olivier and her half-brother Edouard, attends a symbolic dinner given by Profitendieu; and the young Caloub Profitendieu, mentioned in the opening lines of the book, becomes Edouard's new object of interest.

(iii) *Anti-novel or Novel?*

As early as 1914 Gide announced the composition of a large-scale novel, of which *Les Caves du Vatican* was the provisional sketch. In it he proposed to summarize all his thinking on the shortcomings of the nineteenth-century novel – the regular development of a strong central plot, the creation of solid, rounded characters and the predominance of a unifying point of view imposed by the author. As we have shown in our discussion of *Les Caves du Vatican*, Gide considered that such methods led to a gross oversimplification of reality, tending to create the illusion that there was a recognizable 'objective' reality to which all fictional characters must relate and all readers subscribe.

> La vie nous présente de toutes parts quantité d'amorces
> de drames, mais il est rare que ceux-ci se poursuivent et
> se dessinent comme a coutume de les filer un romancier.
> (*Le Journal des Faux-Monnayeurs*, p. 89)[1]

Thus, *Les Faux-Monnayeurs* is an amalgam of many potential novels and dramas corresponding to the different characters involved, sometimes centrally, sometimes tangentially, in the slow unfolding of the principal plot in the fictional scheme, which exists only in a shadowy form until it reaches a rapid climax in the final pages of the novel. Beside the story of Edouard's love affairs, Bernard's attempt to define his attitude to life and Vincent's destructive relationship with Lady Griffith, we note the different personal dramas of Profitendieu, Molinier, Pauline, La Pérouse, Boris, and Laura Douviers, as well as the suggestive allusions to the private lives of Sarah, Rachel and Armand Vedel. Finally, on the outer circumference of the action we glimpse the shadowy figures of Alexandre Vedel, Miss Aberdeen, Gontran de Passavant and Caloub Profitendieu. The whole action is mirrored in Edouard's attempt to come to terms with real life in the search for a 'pure' novel and ends cataclysmically with the fall of the house of Vedel-Azaïs.

Dissatisfied with the arbitrary imposition of a single viewpoint through which the action is seen, Gide adopts a radical solution. There is a marked reduction of third-person narrative elements and a deliberate attempt to create a flat, neutral prose style, stripped of the diverting surface-textures so noticeable in *Les Caves du Vatican*. Anxious to emphasize this illusion of authorial non-intervention, Gide paradoxically intervenes, like Fielding or Sterne, in the final chapter of Part

---

[1] Life presents us on all sides any number of potential dramas, but it is rare for these to be followed up and outlined in the manner of the average novelist. (CDB)

Two to comment on the actions of the characters as though they were completely independent of his control. Events are not viewed directly, therefore, but are slowly and repeatedly uncovered from different angles by those characters that have an interest in them. Inspired by the multiple viewpoint technique of Mérimée, Browning, Conrad and Henry James, Gide juxtaposes different views of the same set of circumstances. This results in the establishment of close connexions between characters and also in the virtual abandonment of a normal time scale.

In Part One, this is particularly noticeable. The eighteen chapters there deal with near simultaneous events taking place on Wednesday afternoon (one and two), Wednesday evening (three to five), Thursday morning (six to eight), Thursday at 11.35 (nine and ten), Thursday afternoon (eleven to fifteen, eighteen) and Thursday evening (sixteen to eighteen). During this time the apparently separate dramas of the immorality case, Bernard's departure from the Profitendieu household and Vincent's connexion with Lady Griffith and Passavant are interwoven with two three-way relationships, Bernard–Olivier–Edouard and Bernard–Laura–Edouard. To achieve this Gide uses a number of indirect techniques – interior monologues, letters, dramatic dialogue and diaries – all linked together by short, economical passages of third-person narrative.

In this way life appears to be an infinite number of unfinished episodes. Juxtaposed chapters seem like a succession of false starts, posing new problems and suggesting alternative directions. Characters are defined in action, through their own characteristic words and thoughts. It is the job of the reader to reconstitute, in collaboration with the author, the connexions between them, as the action shifts almost imperceptibly towards a dramatic climax in Part Three.

Mon livre achevé, je tire la barre, et laisse au lecteur le

soin d'opération; addition, soustraction, peu importe: j'estime que ce n'est pas à moi de la faire. Tant pis pour le lecteur paresseux: j'en veux d'autres.

(*Le Journal des Faux-Monnayeurs*, p. 95)[1]

The reader is, then, the privileged witness of a series of scenes in which characters define themselves and others. In this way he shares in a number of different attempts to come to grips with reality. By means of this dynamic involvement he is forced to acknowledge the existence of a reality which has many facets and where the only connexions possible are the purely arbitrary links proposed by the author.

One stage further in the process of coming to grips with the total aesthetic experience is seen in the views of Edouard on the relationship between literature and life which, in a sense, forms the real subject of the book:

. . . le 'sujet profond' de mon livre. C'est, ce sera sans doute la rivalité du monde réel et de la représentation dont nous nous en faisons. La manière dont le monde des apparences s'impose à nous et dont nous tentons d'imposer au monde extérieur notre interprétation parti-culière, fait le drame de notre vie. (p. 201)[2]

Edouard's theories lead him nowhere, but the novel Gide has written is born of this same tension between appearance and reality, between ideal, artistic truth and banal details drawn from life, between the probable and the fantastic. The desire to work against realism in the direction of 'le roman pur' led

[1] When my book is finished, I draw a line and leave the reader to come to his own conclusion. Addition, subtraction or whatever: in my view, none of this is my job. Too bad if the reader is lazy: I want the other kind. (CDB)

[2] . . . the 'deep-lying subject' of my book. It is – it will be – no doubt, the rivalry between the real world and the representation of it we make to ourselves. The manner in which the world of appearances imposes itself upon us, the manner in which we try to impose on the outside world our own interpretation – this is the drama of our lives. (p. 183)

Gide to an incredible amount of stylization and deliberate artificiality which, as in the great plays of the French classical theatre, creates a world no less true and no less human than that projected in the daily newspapers or the law-reports. In *Les Faux-Monnayeurs* Gide attempted, following the classical dramatists, to arrive at universal, general human truths by concentrating on the specific, individual truth.

This can be seen in the excessively precise focus on the world of the *sixième arrondissement* which is accurate and detailed. Each character is carefully situated in a particular street on different sides of the Luxembourg gardens, but the very precision provides for a more general symbolic connotation. Similarly, some of what one might call the off-stage action takes place in real places like England, Africa and America, but these settings are only vaguely suggested and they are all associated with the distant revolts and damnation of Vincent, Lady Griffith, Sarah and Alexandre. Even Saas-Fée is not described but only evoked as an appropriate place for Bernard's idyllic and unreal relationship with Edouard and Laura.

This refusal to provide consistently realistic descriptions of the various settings contributes to the feeling that the characters move in a quasi-mythical scenario. The action actually takes place in the minds of the characters and the fantastic coincidences and interconnexions, like Bernard's supernatural encounter with the angel, serve to illustrate psychological realities. And when actual physical events take place there is a tendency to concentrate them, either for burlesque or for melodramatic effect (Bernard's offer of help to Laura, Part One, chapter fourteen; the literary banquet, Part Three, chapter eight; Boris's suicide, Part Three, chapter eighteen).

The time-scale of the novel is extremely uneven. Sometimes there is great concentration as in Part One; sometimes it moves swiftly forward a couple of months and is vaguely called 'summer'; or else, as in Part Three, there is a jerky movement from late September to the period of the *baccalauréat* examination and on to the undesignated days leading up to Boris's suicide. There is throughout the novel a further break up of rhythm by the use of retrospective techniques, involving brief allusions to events more distant in time and space.

In opposition to this destruction of the conventional order of the realist novel Gide imposes on the diffuse material a certain patterning or schematization, according to which certain basic relationships are repeated, multiplied or reversed, enabling thematic affirmations to be made and restated. For example, we have noted the analogies between the situation of Laura, Boris and the little girl saved by Lady Griffith from the *Bourgogne*. In addition, there is a succession of inadequate fathers, unsatisfactory marriages and rebellious children. Edouard and Passavant form a contrasting pair: the former, in his role in the destruction of Boris, parallels and contrasts Sophroniska and Strouvilhou. Bernard is paired with Olivier and then with Armand Vedel. The effect of this constant counterpointing is kaleidoscopic.

What is more, the major themes of the novel are concentrated and mirrored in certain symbolic images – the wreck of the *Bourgogne*, the microcosmic world of the Azaïs school, the central image of the counterfeiters. In this way there is a two-way movement: from the apparent formlessness via the elaborate counterpointing to the symbolic 'en abyme' images; from these central images outward to all of the fictional elements with which they can be associated. And in this second shift from central characters like Edouard and Bernard outwards to the characters on the fringe of the action – Vincent, Sarah, Alexandre and finally, Caloub, we have the impression that the progression goes to infinity. Those who deal in false coin are to be found everywhere in society.

Reality is represented by the two shadowy affairs of Dhurmer in Part One and Strouvilhou in Part Three, and the moral implications of these are translated into literary terms in the person of Passavant. Edouard's inability to come to terms with these, despite his possession of special knowledge, coincides with his failure, despite his liberating theories of *inconséquence*, to understand the psychological problems of Boris, thus precipitating the final crisis. Edouard's apparent resentment at the intrusion of Boris's suicide into his settled world is the final pointer to his depiction as a failed novelist.

Gide's novel, on the other hand, is full of life seen at many levels. The allegation is often made that *Les Faux-Monnayeurs*, with its concentration on the articulate members of an upper-class family, is too cerebral by half, too stylized and lacking that sense of real life usually required of a novel. It may be that Gide's main achievement was to make certain technical experiments that were to influence the next two generations of French novelists.

The answer to criticism of this kind can be given only by each individual reader. Certain facts, however, should, in our view, be borne in mind. Firstly, Gide's tampering with the normal time-scale and his replacement of conventional exposition by a succession of juxtaposed points of view do *not* produce an impression of disorder and artificiality. In fact, Gide's discreet use of third-person narrative and his adoption of a relatively neutral style produces an impression of the naturalness he so admired in Stendhal, an ease of manner and a sense of natural growth. Not only is the reader actively involved in the very process of creative fiction and collaborating in the making of a novel; he is also confronted by problems of judgement and perception that closely resemble those he meets every day in real life. For this reason, it is completely wrong to criticize *Les Faux-Monnayeurs* as nothing more than the self-indulgent projection of Gide's own life. There is, in fact, sufficient discretion and blurring of the contours to liberate the reader's imagination and not shackle it to an idiosyncratic view of human nature.

In any case, the book points not to itself: it is through the book that the reader's mind is directed back at life. Gide does not see it as his function to provide reassuring images of life. He is neither conservative, nor escapist, he is uncomfortably provocative:

> Inquiéter, tel est mon rôle. Le public préfère toujours qu'on le rassure. Il en est dont c'est le métier. Il n'en est que trop.
>
> (*Le Journal des Faux-Monnayeurs*, p. 95)[1]

---

[1] It is my business to make people think twice. The public always prefers to be reassured. There are some writers who set out to do just that. There are far too many. (CDB)

6

Social and Political Commitment

For the first half of his adult life Gide had very little time to spend on political and social issues. Born into the *grande bourgeoisie*, brought up in a narrow Protestant background, Gide inherited, on the death of his mother, an extremely large personal fortune, which enabled him to envisage a life devoted to self-study and literature. His principal concern was his individual moral and artistic development. All his energy was directed towards solving the personal and social dilemma posed by his homosexuality and towards the composition of a long list of works in germ in his mind in the 1890s.

During his Symbolist phase, Gide, in common with most of the young disciples of Mallarmé, dreamt of creating works of art divorced from everyday reality. Even when the majority of the French intelligentsia was seething with talk of the Dreyfus Affair, it was only under the influence of Léon Blum that Gide brought himself to voice some vague support for Zola and the revisionists against the nationalist supporters of Barrès and Maurras. He did, however, vigorously question the literary and ethical consequences of right-wing theories when he condemned utilitarian or committed novels in the name of artistic freedom, and mocked Barrès' theory of *enracinement* for the absurd limitations it placed on individual growth and development.

Gide was never attracted to social and moral movements and his fear of commitment to a single group, party or creed owes

much to his distaste for striking attitudes that do not corre-
spond precisely with his innermost feelings and present a false
image of himself to the world. He was always aware, however,
of the social forces that prevented the full expression of his
personality, and tended to identify with social victims, outcasts
and even criminals. Believing his homosexuality to be normal,
he felt that many social taboos were based on a woefully
narrow view of human nature. Hence, his interest in criminal
psychology and the shortcomings of the legal system, where
judgements of human behaviour were made without concern
for underlying psychological factors.

Gide discovered that most eminent professional men gained
an almost automatic exemption from jury-service, and could
usually rely on their local Mayor to remove their names from
the lists. Even after insisting on his availability in 1906 Gide
had to wait six years to be called. His *Souvenirs de la cour
d'assises* (1914) contains many examples of bizarre crimes, none
of which were straightforward, but which were all judged in the
most summary manner by what he dubbed the 'justice-
machine', *la machine-à-rendre-la-justice*. His eye-witness report
of French justice at work was to influence Camus' description
of Meursault's trial in *L'Etranger*, and give rise in 1930 to a
series of published dossiers on controversial cases, under the
title, *Ne jugez pas*.

Gide's alarm at the prejudices of the jury, the crude reliance
on circumstantial evidence and the frequent inability of the
court to unearth hidden motives, led him to a desultory involvement on a personal level with criminals' families. Visiting
the harbour district of Rouen, his mind was opened for the
first time to urban social problems:

> Avant de rentrer me coucher, j'avais longtemps erré dans
> ce triste quartier près du port, peuplé de tristes gens, pour
> qui la prison semble une habitation naturelle – noirs de
> charbon, ivres de mauvais vin, ivres sans joie, hideux.

Et dans ces rues sordides, rôdaient de petits enfants, hâves
et sans sourires, mal vêtus, mal nourris, mal aimés . . .
(*Journal*, II, p. 664)[1]

But Gide's social conscience was not to issue in positive action
for another ten years at least. In 1914 he was appointed
assistant director of the *Foyer franco-belge*, where he worked for
the rehabilitation of Belgian refugees until 1916. From that
time on he became, after a brief flirtation with the right-wing
Action française, increasingly involved with his own religious
problems and his relationship with Marc Allégret. The working
out of these personal problems and the composition of his big
novel, *Les Faux-Monnayeurs*, proved to be major preoccupations until the middle of the 1920s.

The bulk of his social thinking during this period was concentrated on his defence of homosexuality, *Corydon*, which was
completed and then finally published in 1924. In it Gide made
a most courageous stand against the prevailing moral climate,
and to the end of his life he referred to it as his most important
work. Fully conscious that writing and daring to publish such
a work would inevitably bring him to the very opposite of
public acclaim, he took up an aggressive stance. The only
unnatural thing in the world is the work of art: all the rest,
warts and all, is part of nature.

Referring to the latest work in biology and natural history,
Gide set out to prove that the customary assumption that
heterosexuality is normal and homosexuality is an acquired,
unnatural practice has no scientific basis. Biologically speaking,
the female is the centre of gravity of the species and seeks a
heterosexual relationship only for the purpose of reproduction.
This leaves a surfeit of males, especially in the lower orders of

---

[1] Before going home to bed, I had wandered for a long time in this sad
district near the harbour, full of sorry-looking people for whom prison
seems a second home – covered with grime, drunk on bad wine, without
joy, ugly. And in these filthy streets, roamed little children, emaciated
and doleful, ill-clothed, ill-fed, unloved. (CDB)

animal life, and the production of an infinitely greater amount of semen than is strictly needed for procreation. In any case, animals have no instinct for reproducing the species, only an automatic reflex to certain smells emitted by the female. In fact, reproduction is almost an accidental consequence of the search for pleasure that frequently expresses itself among males of the same species.

Nor is homosexuality a modern vice in human society. It flourished in all the great periods of artistic achievement and is in no way inconsistent with the exercise of manly virtues in war and politics. Not only that: homosexuality and lesbianism are more natural and more spontaneous forms of love than heterosexuality. Since love between men and women is calculated to produce children, it is to be relegated below the disinterested expense of sexual energy among homosexuals. Indeed, heterosexual prejudices result from a form of conditioning for social roles without which, Gide confidently asserts, there would be many more practising homosexuals.

It is clear that Gide overstates his case. His is, of course, a committed point of view. In stressing the utilitarian, reproductive role of the heterosexual relationship and reserving the pure and innocent pursuit of physical pleasure for homosexuals, he is really attempting to restore the balance of moral awareness destroyed by centuries of religious prejudice. In the last analysis, he is pleading for a new tolerance for sexuality, and challenging the utilitarian values of bourgeois society in the name of Nature's essential spontaneity and variability.

(ii) *An African Journey*

It is not possible to exaggerate the part played by Gide's contact with Africa in his personal and political development. His six visits to North Africa between 1893 and 1904 had immense personal significance, giving him the freedom to discover the truth about his physical nature. Contact with the people and the landscape produced in Gide a sense of ecstasy and excitement, reflected in the exotic imagery and the resonant harmonies of the intensely lyrical *Nourritures terrestres* and recurring in later works like *L'Immoraliste*, *El Hadj* and *Le Renoncement au Voyage*. He even had the idea of writing a book on economic and social conditions in Algeria, but decided to leave matters of that kind to the experts and pursue his literary vocation.

Gide's rejection of this sort of attitude can already be seen in the opening pages of *Corydon*, which date back to 1910–11, where he claims to speak not as a specialist but from his own experience. The projected book on Algeria, the first draft of *Corydon*, the hints of social awareness in *Souvenirs de la cour d'assises* and the completion of *Corydon* in 1919 form a thin thread of commitment leading to his growing interest in the Russian Revolution, following his study of Dostoevsky and his reading in 1921 of H. G. Wells's articles on Bolshevism. At the same time he became interested in the search for Franco-German co-operation, the policy of Rathenau, whom Gide met in 1921, and Aristide Briand. Furthermore, his reading of Conrad's *Heart of Darkness* – a book about the exploitation of black Africans by white traders – rekindled his earlier desire to write a study of North African problems. A contact in the French Colonial Office agreed to arrange an official visit to French equatorial Africa and, with the completion of *Les Faux-Monnayeurs* in 1925, Gide was ready to leave.

Voyage au Congo and *Le Retour du Tchad* are the records of two journeys made in the company of Marc Allégret between July 1925 and May 1926. Travelling by sea from Dakar to the mouth of the Congo and on to Brazzaville, they then followed the Congo and Oubangui rivers north to Bangui, from where they proceeded by a circuitous route to Lake Tchad. Returning from Lake Tchad, Gide and Allégret journeyed south and west through the Cameroons to the port of Douala, near Fernando Po.

With his major moral and literary problems behind him,

Gide seemed to relive in the Congo the excitement of his first
contact with North Africa:

> Tout m'y charmait d'abord: la nouveauté du climat, de la
> lumière, des feuillages, des parfums, du chant des oiseaux,
> de moi-même aussi parmi cela . . . J'étais grisé.
>
> *(Journal*, II, p. 694)[1]

But this does not herald a return to the exalted lyricism of
Les Nourritures terrestres. Now, Gide's delight in the strange
flora and fauna and the friendliness of the natives is expressed
in a far more restrained, economical poetic prose, almost
Flaubertian in quality.

At the outset Gide emphasizes his desire to remain fair and
objective, and free of anti-colonial prejudices. This is illustrated
by the fact that he continues reading throughout his travels
Shakespeare and Milton, classical French literature, Goethe,
Stevenson and Conrad, not wishing to pose as anything but a
European writer honestly registering his personal impressions.
However, his initial feeling that the natives were happy and
prosperous gradually gives way to an awareness that they are
being shamefully exploited by a fixed-price conspiracy among
freelance rubber merchants, and cruelly treated by the agents
of the rubber companies holding trading concessions from the
French government.

In a dramatic passage nearly half-way through the book
Gide records his discovery of his new commitment to contemporary political problems. From this moment on he will
place his pen at the service of the oppressed native population:

> Quel démon m'a poussé en Afrique? Qu'allais-je donc
> chercher dans ce pays? J'étais tranquille. A présent je sais:
> je dois parler.
>
> *(Journal*, II, p. 745)[2]

[1] Everything delighted me at first – my awareness of the different climate,
light, foliage, smells and birds' songs, as well as my awareness of myself
in the midst of all this . . . I was intoxicated. (CDB)

[2] What demon drove me to come to Africa? What was I searching for in

Despite this, and the many allusions to the ill-treatment of African workers, *Voyage au Congo*, like its sequel, *Le Retour du Tchad*, maintains to the end the status of a travelogue or diary, dominated by long passages describing wild animals, exotic plants, native festivities during meetings with local potentates, as well as Gide's concern for the health of Marc Allégret.

The propagandist implications of Gide's record are to be found in explanatory notes and lengthy appendices to the text, full of statistics, and corroborative evidence. While still on his travels Gide wrote letters to the concessionary companies, and on his return to France launched a campaign in the press, winning the support of leading politicians like Blum and Poincaré. By the early 1930s it was finally decided to modify the system by which trading concessions were allocated to private companies. The immediate consequences of Gide's discovery of the colonial phenomenon were, therefore, limited, but for Gide himself the campaign marked his entry into the political arena.

(iii) *The Communist Adventure*

> La question sociale m'apparaît aujourd'hui la plus importante de toutes et je consens volontiers que l'art subisse, de ce fait, une éclipse prolongée.
>
> *(Littérature engagée*, p. 50)[1]

These words, written in 1934, may sound strange from a man whose whole life had been spent in the elaboration of a personal moral and artistic credo and who, only two or three years later, was to regret the effect of political commitment on his artistic output. They suggest a man wholeheartedly committed to political action and ready to make any sacrifices for it. In

---

this country? My mind lay dormant. Now I know: I must speak out. (CDB)

[1] Social questions seem to me today to be more important than any others and I am perfectly happy that, because of this, literature should suffer a prolonged eclipse. (CDB)

fact, this was not the case. Set in the context of the early 1930s, Gide's words reflect the enthusiasm with which many writers and intellectuals identified with the fight against Fascism. The Fascist riots of 6 February 1934 were followed by a great counter-demonstration by the Radical, Socialist and Communist parties. Intellectuals shared workers' aspirations: the choice was Fascism or fellow-travelling. Most of them felt that they were living in an age of politics.

Gide, as we have seen, had been moving (since 1921) in the direction of social and political involvement, a process completed by the publication of *Voyage au Congo* in 1927. But Gide did not come to Communism by way of the theoretical writings of Marx or Lenin. Like the latter he saw the seeds of the revolutionary spirit in the emphasis in primitive Christianity on poverty and compassion for one's fellow-men. Embarrassed at his own wealth, Gide passionately wanted to identify with the poor and oppressed. Gide saw in the Russian blueprint for the just society an answer to questions he had long been posing.

In 1931, after expressing his enthusiasm for the Soviet Five-Year Plan, he announced his support for Communism, not seeing this as a conversion, but as the logical outcome of his life-long opposition to conventional moral forces. He presided over meetings organized by the Association of Revolutionary Writers and Artists, helped to edit their official organ, *Commune*, and accompanied Malraux to Berlin to intercede with Goebbels in favour of the imprisoned Socialists, Dimitrov and Thaelmann. In his writings there is a constant preoccupation with social matters. In *L'Affaire Redureau* and *La Séquestrée de Poitiers* he produced further evidence to suggest the inability of the legal system to cope with cases where the motivation is not obvious. In a trilogy of works, *L'École des Femmes*, *Robert* and *Geneviève*, he dealt with the role of women in contemporary society, delivering yet another indictment on the bourgeois family. His new faith in the future of Communism found expression in *Les Nouvelles Nourritures*, a copy of which he sent to Moscow in October 1935 with a prefatory address to Russian youth.

At the same time Gide was perfectly aware of the dangers of political commitment. He never joined the Communist party and, in answer to Barbusse's appeal, he stated that he would prefer to remain silent rather than speak under a *diktat* that might inhibit his ability to speak the truth. For there was, Gide felt, no essential contradiction between individualism and Communism. Against the prevailing current of social realism in Russia, he proposed a *Communist individualism*, thus supporting dissidents like Radek, Bukharin and Pasternak. Gide's own experience taught him that great art can never simply mirror the dominant ideology:

> Le grand nombre . . . n'applaudit jamais à ce qu'il y a de neuf, de virtuel, de déconcerté et de déconcertant dans une œuvre: mais seulement à ce qu'il y peut déjà *reconnaître*, c'est-à-dire la banalité. Tout comme il y avait des banalités bourgeoises, il y a des banalités révolutionnaires.
>
> (*Retour de l'U.R.S.S.*, p. 88)[1]

The fears he expressed as early as 1933 about the shortcomings of contemporary Russian society were finally confirmed when he visited Russia in 1936. After pronouncing an oration at the funeral of Maxim Gorky, he toured extensively in Russia, inspecting collective farms, factories and recreation centres and addressing literary clubs, students and working men. He approached his new experiences with the same insistence on objectivity he had shown in *Voyage au Congo* and, although he ascribed many of the faults he found to the naïve enthusiasm of a youthful state, he was dismayed by signs of the

---

[1] The majority never respond to what is new, potentially valuable, to expressions of concern or criticism in a work: it responds only to what it can already recognize there, in other words, what is most banal in it. Just as there used to be bourgeois banalities, there are now revolutionary banalities. (CDB)

growth of a Stalinist orthodoxy that, in his view, betrayed the original aims of the Revolution.

Retour de l'U.R.S.S. is, therefore, more than a simple record of his travels. It articulates his extreme disillusionment at the distance between Communist ideals and the Stalinist reality. Despite Gide's determination to strike a balance between praise and criticism, what comes through time and time again is the grey conformism of Russian society, the acute shortage of retail goods and the progressive re-establishment of 'une aristocratie . . . du bien-pensée, du conformisme, et qui, dans la génération suivante, deviendra celle de l'argent'.[1] (*Retour . . .*, p. 64). Worst of all, he laments the suppression of all unorthodox thought by methods rivalled only by the Nazis.

Gide claims the right to be outspoken because of his love for Russia and his admiration for its achievements. The text is full of asides and brief reminders that he has no technical expertise to speak on certain matters and that, inevitably, his book is an amalgam of personal impressions that he was unable to fully confirm. Statements of this kind border on the disingenuous, for the book is carefully structured to express the distance between ideal and reality. There is a definite shift from uncritical enthusiasm (Part One), to the drabness and shortage of goods noted in Moscow (Part Two), the regimentation of attitudes and the development of a new privileged class (Part Three), the cult of Stalin (Part Four), the absence of artistic freedom (Part Five) and a reminder of the original ideals of the Revolution (Part Six). Furthermore, in Part Three, there is a whole succession of deflationary movements: from Russian pride in the modest hotel at Sotchi to the sordid housing conditions of the construction-workers; from elaborate praise of the hotel near Soukhoumi, via a comic description of chicken-breeding at a model farm, to the inadequate housing of the workers. Thus, Gide's claim to present good and bad, in the

---

[1] An aristocracy based on conformism and the acceptance of prevailing attitudes, which in the next generation will be based on wealth. (CDB)

name of objectivity, does not mask repeated ironic effects of this kind, as one ideal after another is undermined.

The price of Gide's honesty was estrangement from many of his Communist associates, notably Guéhenno, Ilya Ehrenburg and Romain Rolland, with whom he exchanged recriminations that went on until the outbreak of the Second World War. Dubbed a traitor, a Trotskyite and a Fascist, Gide asserted to the last his faith in the humanistic aims of Communism and his attachment to the truth as he saw it:

> Il n'y a pas de parti ... qui me retienne ... et qui me puisse empêcher de préférer, au Parti même, la vérité. Dès que le mensonge intervient, je suis mal à l'aise; mon rôle est de le dénoncer. C'est à la vérité que je m'attache; si le Parti la quitte, je quitte du même coup le Parti.
>
> (*Retouches à mon Retour de l'U.R.S.S.*, p. 67)[1]

[1] No party can completely hold my allegiance and prevent me from preferring truth even to the Party itself. As soon as falsehood appears I am uneasy, because my job is to denounce it. I value truth; if the Party departs from truth, then I immediately take leave of the Party. (CDB)

Conclusion

Gide described himself once as an inn at the crossroads, ready to welcome any newcomer. He saw life as 'un long voyage . . . à travers les livres, les hommes, les pays.'[1] Into his works he poured his total experience of literature and life. At the beginning of his career he embarked on a unique moral and literary quest. Convinced of the variability of his own nature and unwilling to deny expression to any tendency in his mind, he took on the difficult task of manifesting the truth about himself as sincerely as he could. Individual actions representing different psychological, philosophical and aesthetic moments, have to be seen in terms of Gide's grand design, his *œuvre*, his life and work.

With Gide one has the impression of extreme emotional and intellectual power, of excessive self-consciousness and a calculating search for control. For all his advocacy of spontaneity and sincerity, however, does not his mania for self-interrogation deprive him of warmth and humanity? Certainly Brigid Brophy found him too cerebral by half, less prone to sensitivity than to an inability to yield to artistic abandon. We have to remember, of course, that Gide, far from seeking artistic abandon, always strove for understanding and control. It is true that in his deep and wide-ranging analysis of himself and his art Gide betrays a 'scientific' concern for precision, truthfulness and progress. He possessed the scientific instinct all his life: his interest in botany and biology preceded his literary

[1] R. Lang, *André Gide et la Pensée allemande*, Paris, 1949, p. 32 (a long voyage through books, men and countries, CDB).

aspirations. Besides this, he carefully collected psychological and biological data for use in his novels and in order to support his arguments in favour of homosexuality.

Such interests, seen together with his patient literary researches, are evidence of an insatiable intellectual curiosity which Gide illustrates in *Si le grain ne meurt* by recalling his childhood fascination for a kaleidoscope. Whereas his cousins would repeatedly shake the instrument to produce new patterns, the young Gide turned it very slowly in order to examine the slightest change. Out of curiosity he once dismantled it and reassembled it with fewer pieces of glass or with different objects instead of the coloured glass. In this way he spent hours analysing the various effects produced and experienced tremendous excitement at having discovered 'le pourquoi du plaisir' (*Si le grain ne meurt, Journal*, vol. II, pp. 351–2).[1]

Control, then, and clarity, but an equal passion for pleasure and fulfilment. His intellectualism is real but it should not be exaggerated. It is not purely and simply the artistic manifestation of a grotesquely inhibited personality, as Miss Brophy would suggest: it is inseparable from his impulse towards freedom of self-expression and from the desire to come to terms with all sides of his personality. His search for plenitude involved submitting to as much of nature as possible. He is what André Walter aspired to be – 'scientifique et passionné'.[2] The lyrical intensity of *Les Cahiers d'André Walter* and the impression of poetic abandon in *Les Nourritures terrestres*, just like the rich Flaubertian descriptions in *Le Voyage au Congo*, are the artistic results of Gide's deep and spontaneous attachment to life and human experience.

Always a controversial writer, Gide constantly felt that he was writing for future generations. He turned to the past in order to find intellectual nourishment for a future audience.

---

[1] 'how to produce pleasure'. (CDB)

[2] 'scientific and passionate' (CDB). See G. W. Ireland, *André Gide*, Clarendon Press, 1970, pp. 25–30.

His status as a writer, acknowledged by Mallarmé and other writers in the 1890s, depended for many years on a very narrow circle of readers, mainly in the literary intelligentsia. When he did find a wide audience in the 1920s, it was largely as a result of the publicity he received for his defence of homosexuality. His contribution to twentieth-century literature was fully recognized in the final twenty years of his life by the generation of Malraux, Sartre and Camus. Camus saw Gide as one of the great formative influences of his writing as did many later writers. Gide's reappraisal of the novel complements the work of Proust, Joyce and Dos Passos and conditioned the theories of the French 'new novelists', Sarraute, Robbe-Grillet and Claude Simon.

Sartre put his finger on the essential quality of Gide's writings when he spoke of the curious tension that is created by a mixture of courage and prudence we find in them – a combination of provocation and hesitation. With incredible tenacity and devotion Gide pursued the objective he defined in the 1890s, that his philosophy, his ethics and his style must be truly original and new. By emphasizing his own individuality, Gide managed, paradoxically, to live an exemplary life, so that the whole of French thought in the twentieth century had to determine its position in relation to him. This was certainly Gide's secret hope, expressed in allegorical form, in his last work *Thésée*:

> C'est consentant que j'approche la mort solitaire. J'ai goûté les biens de la terre. Il m'est doux de penser qu'après moi, grâce à moi, les hommes se reconnaîtront plus heureux, meilleurs et plus libres. Pour le bien de l'humanité future, j'ai fait mon œuvre. J'ai vécu.[1]

[1] I am quite ready to face death alone. I have tasted the fruits of life. It is reassuring to think that in the future, because of me, men will see that they are happier, better and more free. For the benefit of future humanity I have completed my work. I have lived. (CDB)

Bibliography

A. Basic Reference Works

Gide, André, *Romans, Récits et Soties. Oeuvres lyriques* (Bibliothèque de la Pléiade), Gallimard, 1958. (Contains a useful introduction and notes.)

Gide, André, *Oeuvres complètes*, ed. L. Martin-Chauffier, Nrf, 1932–9.

Cahiers André Gide, Gallimard, 1970– .

Martin, Claude, 'Etat présent des études gidiennes', *Critique*, 206 (1964), pp. 598–625.

Naville, A., *Bibliographie des Ecrits d'André Gide*, H. Matarasso, 1949.

B. Editions of Gide's Works used in this Study

L'Immoraliste (le livre de poche), Mercure de France, 1902.

La Porte étroite (le livre de poche), Mercure de France, 1959.

Les Caves du Vatican (coll. Folio), Gallimard, 1922.

La Symphonie pastorale (coll. Folio), Gallimard, 1925.

Corydon, Gallimard, 1925.

Les Faux-Monnayeurs (coll. Folio), Gallimard, 1925.

Retour de l'U.R.S.S., Gallimard, 1936.

Retouches à mon Retour de l'U.R.S.S., Gallimard, 1937.

Journal, 1899–1939 (Bibliothèque de la Pléiade), Gallimard, 1938.

Journal, 1939–1949. Souvenirs (Bibliothèque de la Pléiade), Gallimard, 1954. (Contains *Si le grain ne meurt* and *Voyage au Congo*.)

C. Translations used in Footnotes in the Present Study

The Immoralist, trans. Dorothy Bussy, Penguin Books, 1960.

Strait is the Gate, trans. Dorothy Bussy, Penguin Books, 1952.

The Vatican Cellars, trans. Dorothy Bussy, Penguin Books, 1952.
La Symphonie pastorale/Isabelle, trans. Dorothy Bussy, Penguin Books, 1963.
The Counterfeiters, trans. Dorothy Bussy, Penguin Books, 1966.

D. Selected Critical Works

I. *General Works*

Archambault, P., *Humanité d'André Gide*, Bloud & Gay, 1946.

Beigbeder, M., *André Gide*, Editions universitaires, 1954.

Boisdeffre, P. de, *La Vie d'André Gide*, Vol. I, Hachette, 1970.

Brée, G., *André Gide, l'insaisissable Protée*, Belles-Lettres, 1953 (available in English version).

Delay, J., *La Jeunesse d'André Gide*, 2 vol., Gallimard, 1956–7 (available in translation).

Guérard, A., *André Gide*, Harvard University Press, 1969.

Hytier, J., *André Gide*, Charlot, 1946 (available in translation).

Ireland, G. W., *André Gide*, Oliver & Boyd, 1963.

Ireland, G. W., *André Gide, a Study of his Creative Writings*, Clarendon Press, 1970.

Lafille, P., *André Gide romancier*, Hachette, 1954.

Littlejohn, D., *Gide: A Collection of Critical Essays*, Prentice-Hall Inc., 1970.

Martin, C., *André Gide par lui-même*, Seuil, 1963.

Moutote, D., *Le 'Journal' de Gide et les Problèmes du Moi*, P.U.F., 1970.

O'Brien, J., *Portrait of André Gide*, Secker & Warburg, 1953.

O'Neill, K., *André Gide and the Roman d'Aventure*, Sydney University Press, 1969.

Rossi, V., *André Gide*, Columbia University Press, 1968.

Savage, C., *André Gide, l'Evolution de sa Pensée Religieuse*, Nizet, 1962.

Starkie, E., *André Gide*, Bowes & Bowes, 1954.

II. *Special Studies*

Bettinson, C. D., *Gide: 'Les Caves du Vatican'*, (Studies in French Literature, 20), Edward Arnold, 1972.

Cancalon, E., *Techniques et Personnages dans les Récits d'André Gide*, Minard, 1970.

Davies, J. C., *Gide: 'L'Immoraliste' and 'La Porte étroite'*, (Studies in French Literature, 12), Edward Arnold, 1968.

Goulet, A., *'Les Caves du Vatican' d'André Gide*, coll. Thèmes et textes, Larousse, 1972.

Idt, G., *André Gide, 'Les Faux-Monnayeurs'*, coll. Profil d'une œuvre, Hatier, 1970.

Lejeune, P., *Exercices d'Ambiguïté, lectures de 'Si le grain ne meurt'* . . ., Minard, 1974.

Martin, C., *André Gide, 'La Symphonie pastorale'*, édition critique, Minard, 1970.

Tolton, C. D. E., *André Gide and the Art of Autobiography. A Study of 'Si le grain ne meurt'*, Macmillan Company of Canada, 1975.

Trahard, P., *'La Porte étroite' d'André Gide. Etude et Analyse*, Editions de la Pensée moderne, 1968.

Wilson, W. D., *A Critical Commentary of 'La Symphonie pastorale'*, Macmillan, 1971.

DATE